ESSENTI

CW00363029

SOUTH AFRICA

Original text by Richard Whitaker
Updated by Philip Briggs

© Automobile Association Developments Limited 2008
First published 2008

ISBN: 978-0-7495-5372-2

Published by AA Publishing, a trading name of Automobile Association Developments
Limited, whose registered office is Fanum House, Basing View, Basingstoke,
Hampshire RG21 4EA.
Registered number 1878835.

Colour separation: MRM Graphics Ltd
Printed and bound in Italy by Printer Trento S.r.l.

A03164
Maps in this title produced from:
map data © New Holland Publishing (South Africa) (PTY) Limited 2007
and © Footprint Handbooks Ltd 2007

About this book

Symbols are used to denote the following categories:

🕂 map reference to maps on cover

✉ address or location

☎ telephone number

🕒 opening times

👋 admission charge

🍴 restaurant or café on premises or nearby

🚇 nearest underground train station

🚌 nearest bus/tram route

🚉 nearest overground train station

⛴ nearest ferry stop

✈ nearest airport

❓ other practical information

ℹ tourist information office

► indicates the page where you will find a fuller description

This book is divided into six sections.

The essence of South Africa
pages 6–19
Introduction; Features; Food and drink and Short break

Planning pages 20–33
Before you go; Getting there; Getting around; Being there

Best places to see pages 34–55
The unmissable highlights of any visit to South Africa

Best things to do pages 56–71
Great place to have cafés; stunning views; places to take the children and more

Exploring pages 72–185
The best places to visit in South Africa, organized by area

Maps
All map references are to the maps on the covers. For example, Barberton has the reference 🕂 23J – indicating the grid square in which it is to be found

Admission prices
Inexpensive (under R20);
Moderate (R10–45);
Expensive (over R50)

Hotel prices
Price are per room per night:
£ budget (under R600);
££ moderate (R600–R1200);
£££ expensive to luxury (over R1200)

Restaurant prices
Price for a three-course meal per person without drinks: £ budget (under R125); ££ moderate (R125–200); £££ expensive (over R200)

Contents

The essence of...

The essence of South Africa lies in the resolve and courage of its people, in its landscapes, flora and fauna, in the edgy vibrancy of its cities. The open plains, the hot bushveld, the mountains and beaches, the baobab trees, the elephants and the lions, have always been there. But because of the willingness of South Africans to talk and compromise – which brought about the democratic transformation of 1994 – far more people than in the past can enjoy these now. At the same time, South Africa's cities are expanding rapidly – shiny new office blocks contrast with sprawling, dusty, shanty towns.

features

What the tourist brochures say about South Africa is true – this really is 'A World in One Country'. You can travel from the Western Cape with its Mediterranean climate, through arid semi-desert areas in the interior, through bushveld and savannah to the subtropical coast of KwaZulu-Natal. You can hike on Table Mountain or in the spectacular uKhahlamba-Drakensberg and drive through the haunting, empty plains of the Karoo. Modern cities such as Cape Town, Johannesburg and Durban contrast with shanty towns and tiny country villages.

The people of this country are one of its greatest strengths. If you smile, acknowledge those you meet and take a minute or two to chat, you will normally encounter enormous friendliness and willingness to help. Remember, however, that many people in South Africa are desperately poor, there are still considerable social problems and crime is a concern – particularly in the inner cities.

For the tourist, South Africa offers many different types of experiences. Soak up the sun on the endless, almost deserted beaches of the Eastern Cape's Wild Coast. Go river-rafting, sea-kayaking or pluck up courage and do the world's highest commercial bungee-jump (216m/ 709ft) from the Bloukrans River bridge. Or enjoy the theatres, cinemas, restaurants and nightclubs in the cities.

Lovers of wildlife can indulge themselves to the full, watching birds in the mountains, forests and wetlands, or going in search of the Big Five – lion, buffalo, elephant, rhino and leopard – in the country's outstanding network of national parks and game reserves.

South Africa is huge, beautiful, mountainous, flat, dry, humid, friendly, sometimes dangerous, but never boring.

GEOGRAPHY

● South Africa is a vast country, covering 1,219,912 sq km (471,108sq miles), with approximately 3,000km (1,860 miles) of coastline.
● Its highest point is the Injisuthi Dome in the uKhahlamba-Drakensberg (3,410m/11,185ft).

LANGUAGES

● South Africa has 11 official languages: Afrikaans, English, Ndebele, Northern Sotho, Southern Sotho, SiSwati, Tsonga, Tswana, Venda, isiXhosa and isiZulu.
● English is commonly used for official purposes.

ECONOMY

● The major sectors are mining, agriculture and fishing, manufacturing industries and, increasingly, tourism.

PEOPLE

Archbishop Tutu has rightly called South Africa the 'Rainbow Nation'. The largest part of the 'rainbow' is the black African majority. Indigenous Bushmen (San) and Khoikhoi ('Hottentot'), Dutch settlers, Indonesians originally brought to the Cape as slaves, settlers from England and other European countries and immigrants from elsewhere in Africa, make up the rest of the spectrum.

food & drink

South Africa's indigenous and immigrant population, and its diversity of climates, have created the country's varied culinary traditions. Imported recipes, adapted over the centuries with the inclusion of local ingredients and innovative cooking methods, have given it its originality.

AFRICAN CUISINE

Traditional staples are meat *(nyama)*, usually roasted or boiled, a white porridge *(pap)* made from maize, and wild spinach (Zulu *imifino*, Sotho *morogo*). Nowadays the *pap* is often eaten with a spicy stew of meat, onions, tomatoes and peppers. Mopani worms, dried caterpillars of the emperor moth, are an acquired taste.

IMMIGRANT CUISINE

Most of the international types of food – Indian, Chinese, French, Italian, British – can be found in the cities. The Portuguese in Southern Africa have developed their own distinctive style of chicken and seafood dishes spiced with peri-peri, a concoction of chillies and peppers.

INDONESIAN (MALAY) & AFRIKANER CUISINE

So-called 'Cape Malay' slaves, mainly from Indonesia, had a very strong influence on Dutch and then Afrikaner cooking, resulting in many of the foods now thought of as typically South African. Among these are delicious *bredies*, stews of vegetables and/or meat – best known are those made with tomatoes or *waterblommetjies*, a kind of water lily. Other specialties are *bobotie*, made with curried minced or ground meat and egg, *sosaties* (spicy kebabs), *konfyt* (a range of sweet fruit preserves), and *blatjang* (tasty fruit chutney). For sweets try *koeksisters*, twisted deep-fried doughnuts, dipped in syrup.

BARBECUES AND MEATS

The barbecue *(braai)* is a South African institution. Expect to eat quantities of grilled steak, chops, kebabs, chicken and, above all, *boerewors*, a sausage of coarse-ground spiced meat. Typical accompaniments are a green salad and beer.

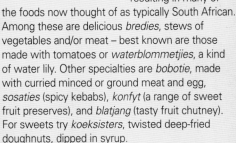

Unusual meats can be found at some restaurants: game of various kinds, such as springbok, impala, kudu and warthog, as well as ostrich, now quite common, and guineafowl. A great local favourite is *biltong*, dried and seasoned meat – usually beef or game.

SEAFOOD

In most coastal cities and towns you can find excellent fresh seafood. The West Coast specializes in lobsters and mussels. Try Cape salmon, firm-fleshed *kabeljou* (kob), *perlemoen* (abalone – if you're lucky enough to find it), octopus and calamari in the Western Cape. The town of Knysna is renowned for its delicious fresh oysters, while the East Coast, especially Durban, is famous for its fine shrimp.

FRUIT

The country's various climatic zones produce fresh fruit of all kinds: in the subtropical northeast, pawpaws, mangos and bananas;

PUB LUNCHES OSTRICH STEAK MEALS

on the highveld and lowveld of Mpumalanga, oranges, grapefruit and *naartjies* (tangerines); in the southwest, grapes and deciduous fruits such as apples and apricots. For something unusual, try the peeled fruit of the prickly pear in the Eastern Cape.

DRINK

The best-known traditional African drinks are *tshwala*, a thick beer made from fermented sorghum and water, and *amasi*, a yoghurt-like drink of thick curdled milk.

The Western Cape, with its Mediterranean climate, has been making wine for more than 300 years, and now exports it all over the world. Because of the relatively

hot summers, the reds are strong and full-bodied, the most popular types being cabernet sauvignon, shiraz, merlot and the local pinotage. The white wines – most abundantly, Chenin blanc, sauvignon blanc and chardonnay – have a crisp, slightly fruity flavour. Good fortified wines and brandy are also made locally.

short break

If you only have a short time to visit South Africa, or would like to get a really complete picture of the country, here are some of the essentials:

● **Swim at Plettenberg Bay** from some of the most beautiful, golden beaches in the world (➤ 42).

● **Take a trail through a game reserve.** Walk with a seasoned ranger, camp in the bush and see South Africa's wildlife up close.

- **Buy local art** South African art is a fascinating hybrid of African and international styles. Buy from a gallery, or bargain with the hawkers on the street corners or at the many open-air markets.

- **Visit a township** on an organized tour or with a resident you know. Created under apartheid for urban blacks, the townships are where the majority of South Africa's city-dwellers live.

- **Go down a gold mine.** Experience first hand what hundreds of thousands of men have gone through to produce the country's premier export.

- **Travel long-distance by train.** This is a wonderful way to take in the countryside while getting from one city to the next. You can ride in expensive luxury on the Blue Train or Rovos Rail, or cheaply on the ordinary trains.

- **Enjoy a *braai* (barbecue).** South Africans love to cook out in the open air. Get to know the locals and you're almost certain to be invited to one.

● **Visit a vineyard** in the Western Cape, taste the wines (and the cheeses that many farms also produce) and enjoy a leisurely lunch under the oak trees (➤ 58).

● **Listen to music at a jazz club.** Some of the world's finest jazz musicians started out in the local clubs. Experience their vibrant atmosphere, and perhaps get a sneak preview of the next international star.

● **Canoe or raft the Gariep River** and experience the ultimate in peace and quiet. At night you will see more stars than you've ever seen before (➤ 174).

Planning

Before you go

WHEN TO GO

JAN	FEB	MAR	APR	MAY	JUN	JUL	AUG	SEP	OCT	NOV	DEC
21°C	21°C	20°C	18°C	15°C	13°C	12°C	13°C	14°C	16°C	18°C	20°C
70°F	70°F	68°F	64°F	59°F	55°F	54°F	55°F	57°F	61°F	64°F	68°F

🔵 High season 🔵 Low season   Average weather conditions for Cape Town

Climatically, seasons are the reverse of Europe, with summer running from October to April and winter from June to September. Most of the country has a summer rainfall pattern, the exception being the Western Cape (including Cape Town), which typically enjoys long, sunny, rainless summer days, but can be downright soggy in winter. By contrast, the Kruger Park and coastal parts of KwaZulu-Natal become uncomfortably hot and humid in midsummer, but tend to be idyllic in winter, with warm, dry days giving way to crisp comfortable evenings.

Game viewing is most productive during August to October, when the vegetation has thinned out. For birdwatchers, November to March is the prime season, as many species begin to breed and resident bird populations are boosted by Eurasian and intra-African migrants.

WHAT YOU NEED

● Required
○ Suggested
▲ Not required

Some countries require a passport to remain valid for a minimum period (usually at least six months) beyond the date of entry – check before you travel.

	UK	Germany	USA	Netherlands	Spain
Passport	●	●	●	●	●
Visa (regulations can change – check before booking your journey)	▲	▲	▲	▲	●
Onward or return ticket	●	●	●	●	●
Health inoculations	○	○	○	○	○
Health documentation (▶ 23, Health Insurance)	▲	▲	▲	▲	▲
Travel insurance	●	●	●	●	●
Driving licence (national)	●	●	●	●	●
Car insurance certificate	●	●	●	●	●
Car registration document	●	●	●	●	●

WEBSITES

www.sanparks.org
www.sa-venues.com
www.southafrica.com

www.southafrica.info
www.southafrica.net
www.backpackingsouthafrica.co.za

TOURIST OFFICES AT HOME

In the UK

South African Tourism
6 Alt Grove
Wimbledon
London SW19 4DZ
☎ 020 8971 9350 or 0870 1550044

20th Floor
Suite 2040
New York NY 10110
☎ 212 730 2929 or 1-800-593-1318

In Australia

South African Tourism
Suite 301, Level 3,
117 York Street,
Sydney NSW 2000.
☎ +61 2 9261 5000

In the USA

South African Tourism
500 Fifth Avenue

HEALTH INSURANCE

Medical insurance inclusive of full repatriation cover is strongly recommended. Hospitals and other medical facilities in South Africa are good and relatively affordable but costs are not covered by the state – bills must be paid for privately and treatment may be withheld if you are uninsured and have no evidence of means to pay. Your medical insurance cover should include dental treatment.

TIME DIFFERENCES

| GMT 12 noon | South Africa 2PM | Germany 1PM | USA (NY) 7AM | Netherlands 1PM | Spain 1PM |

South African Standard Time is 2 hours ahead of Greenwich Mean Time (GMT+2), so only one hour ahead of Britain during British summer time. The whole country lies within the same time zone. But the Western Cape, lying furthest to the south and west, has long summer evenings.

NATIONAL HOLIDAYS

1 January *New Year's Day*
21 March *Human Rights Day*
March/April *Good Friday*
March/April *Family Day* (Monday after Easter Sunday)
22 April *Freedom Day*
1 May *Workers Day*

16 June *Youth Day*
9 August *National Women's Day*
24 September *Heritage Day*
16 December *Day of Reconciliation*
25 December *Christmas Day*

26 December *Day of Goodwill*

Public holidays apply to all workers. School holidays: mid-December to late January (6 weeks); Easter (4 weeks); July–August (5 weeks).

WHAT'S ON WHEN

January A different Shakespeare play is produced each year in the beautiful outdoor setting of Maynardville Park, Wynberg, Cape Town. ☎ 021-421 7695; www.oldwynberg.co.za

February *Cape Town Pride Festival:* South Africa's most prominent gay and lesbian event runs over ten days, culminating in a street parade through Green Point ☎ 021-425 6461; www.capetownpride.co.za

March *Vintage Tractor Show:* Farmers from all over the region bring their antique machines to the unique held during the first week of March at Sandstone Estate, Ficksburg in the Free State. ☎ 051-933 2130

April *Rand Easter Show:* An annual festival held in Johannesbury for 10 days around Easter, it's a huge mix of trade exhibitions and demonstrations, specialty events and fairground rides ☎ 011-661 4000; www.randshow.co.za

Splashy Fen: Situated on a farm near Underberg, this popular music festival offers three stages of ongoing mainstream and alternative rock and pop acts ☎ 033-701 1932; www.splashyfen.co.za

June *National Arts Festival:* From the last week in June, for 10 days, Grahamstown comes alive with Southern Africa's biggest arts festival. Features are music, dance, drama and visual arts from Africa and the rest of the world. ☎ 046-603 1103; www.nafest.co.za

July *The Knysna Oyster Festival:* Dedicated to the town's best-known culinary treat, this is a feast of oyster-related activities and performing arts ☎ 044-382 5510; www.oysterfestival.co.za

August *Oppikoppi Music Festival:* One of the country's biggest music festivals, featuring up to 80 local rock bands performing in the bushveld, about two hours from Johannesburg ☎ 012-346 2011; www.oppikoppi.co.za

September *Arts Alive* in Johannesburg showcases local and international music, dance and theatre ☎ 011-838 9145; www.artsalive.co.za

North West Cultural Calabash in the remote village of Taung has become a major annual showcase for African performing arts ☎ 018-392 4100; www.sa-venues.com

Woodstock: Four-day music festival held at Hartebeespoort Dam, north of Johannesburg ☎ 011-646 6467; www.woodstock.co.za

October *Hermanus Whale Festival:* The arrival of the whales is celebrated with live music, a craft market, and arts and environmental activities ☎ 028-313 0928; www.whalefestival.co.za

Poetry Africa: Durban's annual celebration of poetry, with participants from many countries ☎ 031-260 2506; www.ukzn.ac.za/cca/Poetry_Africa.htm

November *Spier Festival:* From November until the end of March, Cape Town offers music, opera and drama in an open-air theatre on the beautiful Spier Wine Estate ☎ 021-809 1111; www.speierarts.org.za

Cherry Festival: Ficksburg in the Free State celebrates the blooming of its thousands of cherry trees late in November ☎ 051-933 6486; www.cherryfestival.co.za

December *Oude Libertas Summer Festival:* In Stellenbosch begins in December and runs till March, offering drama, dance, opera and music in a graceful open-air auditorium ☎ 021-809 7473

Getting there

BY AIR

Johannesburg Airport

25 kilometres to city centre

🚆 N/A minutes

🚌 35 minutes

🚗 35 minutes

Cape Town Airport

22 kilometres to city centre

🚆 N/A minutes

🚌 20 minutes

🚗 20 minutes

Most major European and African airlines fly to South Africa. The national carrier South African Airways operates a global network of flights, and its website (www.flysaa.com) is worth checking for discounts. The main hub for international flights is OR Tambo (formerly Johannesburg) International Airport, which lies 30–45 minutes from central Johannesburg and the popular suburb of Sandton, an hour or so from Pretoria, and 4–5 hours from the Kruger National Park. An increasing number of international carriers touch down at Cape Town or Durban's international airports, or you can book one of the domestic flights that connect these major centres daily.

South Africa borders six other southern African countries: Namibia, Zimbabwe, Botswana, Mozambique, Swaziland and Lesotho (the last being contained entirely within South Africa). The Vioolsdrift border with Namibia and Beit Bridge border with Zimbabwe stay open 24 hours, while other major border posts such as Kopfontein (Botswana), Lebombo (Mozambique), Oshoek (Swaziland) and Tela Bridge (Lesotho) are generally open from 6–7am to 10pm, but minor border posts generally keep shorter hours, typically 8am–4pm. Regular flights connect major cities in South Africa to the capital and other major tourist hubs in neighbouring countries, and long-distance buses are operated by the likes of Greyhound and Intercape. Rail services run to several borders, but they are not tourist class and do not actually cross the border.

Getting around

PUBLIC TRANSPORT

Internal flights There is an excellent domestic network serving all the cities, some of the main tourist sights and a number of the smaller towns. A recent proliferation of domestic carriers has resulted in a massive drop in prices, and bargains are often available online – try Kulula (www.kulula.com), One Time (www.1time.co.za), Nationwide (www.flynationwide.co.za) or South African Airways (www.flysaa.com).

Trains Tourist class trains are safe, comfortable and good value, but they only run along four routes: Johannesburg to Durban, to Port Elizabeth and to Cape Town, and Cape Town to Durban via Port Elizabeth. The economy class trains that service other routes are more basic and less safe, but even better value. Details of all intercity rail services are listed under the 'Passenger' section of www.spoornet.co.za. Trains are very slow but tourist class carriages offer sheets and blankets and old-fashioned meals in a dining car. The luxury Blue Train runs between Cape Town and Pretoria.

Buses Long-distance buses offer a popular form of travel and all intercity routes are serviced. Fares are very cheap by international standards and availability is seldom a problem with a few days' notice, but it is necessary to book in advance, which is most easily done online. The four main operators are Greyhound (www.greyhound.co.za), Intercape (www.intercape.co.za). Intercity Express (www.intercity.co.za) and Translux (www.translux.co.za). Baz Bus (www.bazbus.co.za) is a hop-on, hop-off service between selected hostels in most parts of the country.

Urban Transport Very little public transport is suitable for tourists in the cities, except for the suburban railway in Cape Town and the Mynah shuttle in Durban.

FARES AND TICKETS

Most flights and coach services can be booked online using a credit or debit card. Few concessions are available. A useful booking agency for transport, theatres, cinemas etc is www.computicket.com.

TAXIS

In South Africa, the term 'taxi' is most often used to refer to one of the multiplying armada of minibus 'taxis' that serve as the main form of urban and intercity public transport throughout the country. Though inexpensive, these taxis are noisy and often overloaded, and the ranks they leave from often attract pickpockets and other thieves, so they cannot be recommended to visitors except on familiar main routes. Metered charter taxis, widely referred to as cabs or minicabs, can be summoned by phone (any hotel will arrange this) or caught at a taxi stand, but may not be hailed in the street.

DRIVING

- South Africans drive on the left.
- Speed limit on freeways: 120kph (74mph)
- Speed limit on rural roads: 100kph (62mph)
- Speed limit in built-up areas: 60kph (37mph)
- Seatbelts are compulsory for drivers and front-seat passengers.
- Never drive under the influence of alcohol. Random breath testing, primarily in urban areas. Drunken driving is severely punished.
- Unleaded petrol, lead-replacement petrol (LRP) and diesel are widely available and relatively inexpensive, but must be paid for with cash – neither credit/debit cards nor cheques are accepted. There are stretches of open road where you might go 100km (60 miles) without passing a filling station, so plan ahead.
- The British AA/RAC has reciprocal arrangements with other national driving associations and will give advice and travel information and arrange emergency breakdown services. Be wary of tow trucks, whose operators sometimes charge exorbitant rates.

CAR RENTAL

The usual international car rental firms have offices throughout the country and offer good service. Local firms offer a cheaper rate but a more limited service. Car rental is expensive and it is advisable to shop around for deals. Bear in mind the huge distances to be covered, and check for unlimited mileage offers. Ensure you have a full set of tools and spares before setting out.

Being there

TOURIST OFFICES

- Western Cape Tourism (including Cape Town)
  Pinnacle Building, Corner of Berg and Castle streets,
  Cape Town 8000
  ☎ 021-426 5639;
  www.tourismcapetown.co.za

- Durban Tourist Junction
  Old Station Building,
  160 Pine Street, Durban
  ☎ 031-304 4934;
  www.kzn.org.za

- Johannesburg Tourism
  Ground Floor Grosvenor Corner
  195 Jan Smuts Avenue
  Johannesburg 2001

- ☎ 011-214 0700;
  www.joburgtourism.com

- Mpumalanga Tourism
  N4 Halls Gateway
  Mpumalanga Parks Board Complex, Nelspruit
  ☎ 013-752 7001;
  www.mpumalanga.com

- Free State Tourism
  Bojanala Building, 34 Markgraaf St, Bloemfontein, 9300 ☎ 086 110 2185; www.dteea.fs.gov.za

- North West Province Tourism
  ☎ 012-386 1225;
  www.tourismnorthwest.co.za

MONEY

The monetary unit is the Rand, divided into 100 cents. R10, R20, R50, R100 and R200 notes are available. Major credit cards are widely accepted. Most banks have exchange facilities but will require your passport for identification. MasterCard holders may use any Thomas Cook network location to report loss or theft, and to obtain an emergency card.

TIPS/GRATUITIES

Yes ✓ No ✗		
Restaurants (if service not included)	✓	10–15%
Tour guides (per day)	✓	R20–R30
Bar service	✗	
Taxis	✓	R5
Porters (per item)	✓	R2
Chambermaids	✓	R5–R10

POSTAL AND INTERNET SERVICES

South Africa has a relatively inexpensive and reliable postal service, but losses are more frequent than in most Western countries, and international delivery frequently takes up to two weeks. If speed or security are a high priority, it is advisable to use an international courier service. Post offices are generally open 8am–4pm on weekdays and 8am–noon on Saturdays. All post offices have public phones attached and phone cards are available. Internet has taken off in a big way in South Africa, and inexpensive facilities are available at most international quality hotels, as well as at internet cafés in most towns of any size.

TELEPHONES

The telephone service is good and many public phones have been installed recently. Phone cards for the green public call boxes are available in most cafés and pubs. Mobile or cell phones with international roaming facilities should work in South Africa, but if you expect to call or text (SMS) home regularly or to use your mobile extensively within South Africa, it's probably worth buying an inexpensive local SIM card to insert in your phone, and making use of the 'pay as you go' service offered by providers such as MTN or Vodacom.

The international dialling code for South Africa is 27. International direct dial is 09 followed by the country code. As of Jan 2007, the full ten-digit number including the area code (eg 011-888 8888) must always be dialled, even from a number with an identical area code.

International Dialling Codes
Dial 09 followed by
UK: 44
Germany: 49
Canada: 1
USA: 1
Netherlands: 31

Emergency Telephone Numbers
Police (Flying Squad): 10111
Fire: 1022 (ask for fire)
Ambulance: 10177 (ask for ambulance)

EMBASSIES AND CONSULATES

Australia ☎ 012-342 3740
UK ☎ 012-483 1200
Germany ☎ 012-427 8900
Netherlands ☎ 012-344 3910
Spain ☎ 012-364 3875
US ☎ 012-342 1048

HEALTH ADVICE

Medical treatment In larger towns doctors are listed in the telephone directory under Medical Practitioners. All hospitals have a 24-hour emergency service and most family doctors have a designated after hours practitioner. The number will be on the answer machine of the regular practice.

AIDS is endemic, with some 15 per cent of the sexually active population estimated to be HIV positive. Condoms are readily available. Blood for medicinal purposes is carefully screened and treated.

Dental services Dentists are listed in the telephone book under Medical Practitioners. There is usually a number on the answer machine for emergencies that occur after hours.

Sun advice Wear a hat and high-factor sun block and stay in the shade in the intense midday heat. Remember to keep up your liquid intake. If you become dehydrated, take a cool bath and drink plenty of water.

Medication All cities and main towns have pharmacies and dispensing pharmacists who will advise you on appropriate medication. Malaria is endemic in the northern and northeastern parts of the country. You must start using the appropriate medication a week before you plan to visit a malarial area and continue for 4–5 weeks after you have left.

Safe water Tap water is safe. In bush camps check before drinking. Purify water from rivers and lakes (boiling/purification tablets). Mineral water is readily available. It is adisable to swim only in populated areas.

PERSONAL SAFETY

Most South African cities have a security problem. Central Cape Town and Durban require a fairly high level of vigilance during daylight hours, while parts of Johannesburg are virtual no-go areas. The first rule is to try not to look affluent. Don't walk the streets festooned with cameras and jewellery; if you must carry valuables, put them in an old shopping bag. Use credit cards and travellers' cheques where possible and avoid carrying large amounts of cash. Do not walk alone after dark; take a taxi instead. If you are mugged, hand over your valuables and do not resist. Wait until your assailant is out of sight and then call the police. Keep car windows and doors locked and do not pick up hitchhikers or stop to help people; phone the police instead. Always park in well lit and preferably busy places. Many parking areas are manned by private guards who will watch

your car, but will expect a tip when you return (anything from R1 to R5, depending on how long you were parked).
Police assistance:
☎ 10111 from any call box

ELECTRICITY

220–230 volts AC 50Hz. Sockets take three round pins. Adaptors for square pins are available but may be in short supply. Power is reliable in towns, but may be intermittent in remote areas, where it is advisable to bring a flashlight. US appliances may need a transformer.

OPENING HOURS

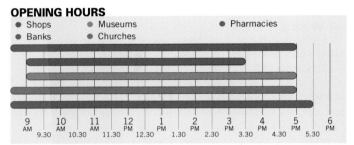

- Shops
- Banks
- Museums
- Churches
- Pharmacies

| 9 AM | 10 AM | 11 AM | 12 PM | 1 PM | 2 PM | 3 PM | 4 PM | 5 PM | 6 PM |
| 9.30 | 10.30 | 11.30 | 12.30 | 1.30 | 2.30 | 3.30 | 4.30 | 5.30 | |

The vast majority of shops, offices, banks, tourist sites and places of worship are open at least from 9am–4:30pm weekdays, and many shops open later. Most offices are closed over weekends, but banks open from 9–11am on Saturday. Particularly in the cities, many shops now operate normal opening hours on Saturday and slightly shortened hours on Sunday. In almost any town you'll find at least one corner or garage shop stays open until around 9pm daily. Museum times vary greatly so check the individual listings. Larger towns generally have at least one 24-hour pharmacy; check the phone book or ask your hotel reception.

LANGUAGE

South Africa has 11 official languages, but you can generally get by in English in cities and at established tourist attractions. In rural areas and small towns all over the country Afrikaans is widely used. Although for practical purposes you are unlikely to need to use the African languages, you will meet with a very friendly response if you attempt some of the basic words and phrases listed below. isiXhosa is spoken in the Western and Eastern Cape, and understood in KwaZulu-Natal; although isiZulu is the most widely spoken language in this region. Sesotho is spoken in the Free State, Gauteng and much of the Limpopo Province. Siswati is spoken in Swaziland while isiXhosa is the language of the Eastern Cape. Setswana is spoken in the Northen Cape and the Northwest Province.

English	Afrikaans	isiZulu	isiXhosa
Hello	Hallo	Sawubona	Molo (good morning) Rhoananai (good evening)
Goodbye	Totsiens	Sala kahle	Sala sentle
How are you?	Hoe gaan dit?	Ninjani?	Kunjani?
Fine, thank you	Goed, dankie	Hgisaphila	Ndiphilile, enkosi
Please	Asseblief	Uxolo	Nceda
Thank you	Dankie	Ngiyabonga	Enkosi
Yes	Ja	Yebo	Ewe
No	Nee	Cha	Hayi
Excuse me	Verkoon my	Uxolo	Uxolo

English	Setwana	Sesotho	Siswati
Hello	Dumela	Dumela	Sawubona
Goodbye	Sala sentle	Sala Hantle	Salakahle
How are you?	O tsogile jang?	O kae?	Ninjani?
Fine, thank you	Ke tsogile sentle	Ke phela hantle	Kulungile
Please	Tsweetswee	(Ka kopo) hle	Ngicela
Thank you	Ke a leboga	Ke a leboha	Ngiyabonga
Yes	Ee	E	Yebo
No	Nnyaa	The	Cha
Excuse me	Intshwarele	Ntschwaerele	

Useful words in Afrikaans

Bill	Rekening	Left	Links
Cheap	Goedkoop	Petrol/Gasoline	Brandstoff
Expensive	Duur	Police	Polisie
Exit	Uitgang	Right	Regs
Good/nice	Lekker	Ticket	Kaartjie

Best places to see

1 Blyde River Canyon

The Blyde River Canyon is a place of superb views, soaring peaks, caves, waterfalls and a challenging hiking trail.

Some of South Africa's finest scenery can be found along the escarpment in Mpumalanga, where the interior plateau (the Highveld) drops away to the subtropical plains below (the Lowveld). Over the past 60 million years the Blyde River has carved its

way through the Escarpment to form a canyon 300–800m (984–2,624ft) deep.

The Blyde River Canyon proper is a nature reserve offering bird-watching, numerous walking and riding trails, restaurants and camping in designated areas. A two-day hiking route of 40km (25 miles) runs the length of the canyon, next to the river, but it is the spectacular views and sights near the canyon and along its rim that are the main attractions of the area. The Mac Mac Falls plunge 85m (280ft) into a bushy gorge near the Mac Mac Pools, a descending series of natural basins. Also worth a visit are the 46m (150ft) Berlin Falls, on a stream that runs into the Blyde River. At **Bourke's Luck Potholes,** at the confluence of the Treur and Blyde rivers, you can view rocks scoured over the millennia into weird shapes by waterborne debris.

The God's Window and Wonder View look-out points provide magnificent panoramas from the edge of the escarpment over the Lowveld eastwards as far as the Kruger National Park (► 46–47). Don't miss the view of the Three Rondavels, a group of hills towering over the canyon, named for their resemblance to thatched huts.

If you're not claustrophobic, visit the **Echo Caves,** where the stalactites resound eerily when struck.

🕂 23K

Bourke's Luck Potholes

✉ About 37km (22 miles) north of Graskop, Mpumalanga ☎ 013-761 1377 🕒 Daily 7–5 ✋ Inexpensive 🍴 Kiosk (£) ✈ Fly to

Johannesburg
❓ Panorama
Tourism Board
☎ 013-767 1377
Echo Caves
☎ 013-238 0015
🕒 Daily 8:30–4:30
✋ Moderate
🍴 Restaurant (££)

2 # Cape Peninsula and Table Mountain

www.tmnp.co.za

The Cape Peninsula and Table Mountain National Park offer extraordinary variety – beaches, mountains, wild animals – in the middle of a major city.

Cape Town must be one of the few major cities in the world whose residents can spend the morning hiking along beautiful mountain footpaths and the

afternoon lounging around on an idyllic beach. The city surrounds the wilderness of Table Mountain, which stands sentinel above the city centre, its flat top easily reached by cable car, except when it is shrouded in a 'tablecloth' of fluffy clouds.

At many points the mountain drops away to a coastline indented to form beautiful sandy coves and bays. The best beaches for swimming are on False Bay (Muizenberg, Fish Hoek, The Boulders), where the water is several degrees warmer than on the western side of the Peninsula. The beaches at Clifton and Camps Bay, where the water is colder, are scenic and ideal for sunbathing.

Cape Town forms part of the Cape Floral Kingdom, a UNESCO World Heritage Site renowned for its unique heath-like vegetation known as fynbos (fine bush). It is by far the smallest of the world's six floral kingdoms, but also the most richly diverse, with 70 per cent of its 9,600 plant species found nowhere else on earth. The Cape Peninsula alone has 2,300 species.

Table Mountain National Park extends over 25,000 ha (61,750 acres) and incorporates the former Cape Of Good Hope Nature Park, the fantastically scenic southern tip of the peninsula, also known as Cape Point. A network of paths criss-cross the park, from Table Mountain to Cape Point. But be warned: several tourists have to be rescued from the mountain each year. Take a map, water and warm clothing – even in summer.

✚ 2A and 27T ✉ Cape Town, Western Cape
ℹ Corner of Castle and Burg streets, Cape Town
☎ 021-426 4260

3 Cradle of Humankind

www.maropeng.co.za

Designated as a UNESCO World Heritage Site in 1999, the so-called Cradle Of Humankind (CoH) consists of around 20 different dolomite caves set in a patchwork of disjointed conservancies that sprawls across 130,000 ha (321,100 acres) to the northwest of Johannesburg.

The world's greatest known concentration of hominid (human-like) fossils has been recovered in these caves, representing a near continuum of hominid habitation stretching back some 3.5 million years, and the site has also produced a remarkable wealth of stone tools. It should be clarified, however, that the CoH is not (as many suppose) where the oldest-known hominid remains have been unearthed – that distinction belongs to Afar in the Ethiopian Rift Valley and/or the Lake Chad basin.

The main tourist focus is the Sterkfontein Caves, which lie on the outskirts of Krugersdorp, about 45km (27 miles) northwest of central Johannesburg. This is where, back in 1936, Dr Robert Broom uncovered the first known fossil of an adult 'ape-man', popularly dubbed Mrs Ples, and it has since yielded a number of other fascinating palaeontological discoveries. A visit to Sterkfontein is easily combined with (and arguably best preceded by) a stop at nearby Maropeng ('Place of Origin'), where a two-hour self-guided tour of the architecturally innovative visitors' centre helps to place the discoveries at Sterkfontein and elsewhere in the CoH in perspective. With time to

spare, you could extend your exploration of the area to the pretty Krugersdorp Game Reserve, about 15 minutes' drive from Sterkfontein Caves.

For further insight into human evolution and cultural development, visit the Museum of Origins at the University of Witwatersrand in Braamfontein, immediately north of central Johannesburg.

✚ 20J ✉ Western Gauteng, bordering Northwest Province
☎ 014-577 9000; www.maropeng.co.za (Maropeng) or
011-668 3200; www.sterkfontein-caves.co.za (Sterkfontein
Caves) 🕐 Daily 9–5 🖐 Expensive 🍴 Restaurant (££)

4 Garden Route

www.gardenroute.co.za

One of South Africa's greatest tourist attractions, the Garden Route runs along the coast of the southeastern Cape through forests, lakes and farmland.

The Western Cape's Garden Route extends along the coast from Mossel Bay in the west to the Tsitsikamma Forest in the east, with the Outeniqua Mountains forming the northern border of this popular tourist area.

Driving east on the N2 from Mossel Bay you pass a superb beach at Glentana before cutting inland through rolling green fields to the country town of George. From here the N2 leads on to the resort of Wilderness, set in the middle of an extensive lakeland and wetland system. Accommodation of all types is available here – caravans, houseboats, campsites, chalets, bed-and-breakfasts and farms offering home stays. Next is the lovely town of **Knysna,** lying along the shores of a large lagoon. Shop here for items made from indigenous hardwoods, and enjoy the locally produced beer and oysters.

At the heart of the Garden Route is **Plettenberg Bay** ('Plett' for short), originally, and aptly, called Baia Formosa (Beautiful Bay) by the Portuguese. You can swim from golden beaches or take a boat trip to view dolphins, seals and whales.

East of Plettenberg Bay, after crossing the soaring Bloukrans River Bridge, you come to the Tsitsikamma Forest, well worth a detour. Along this stretch are the famous 800-year-old Big Tree (a giant

yellowwood) which is 37m (121ft) tall, and the resorts of Nature's Valley and Storms River Mouth.

Adventure activities are available all along the Garden Route, including sea-kayaking, canoeing, hiking, mountain biking and paragliding. If you're particularly adventurous, try the world's highest commercial bungee jump (216m/700ft) from the Bloukrans River Bridge (expensive).

The Garden Route is very popular with locals as well as tourists, so reservations are essential during the high season (December to January).

✚ 5A–6B ✉ Southeast coast of Western Cape
✈ Fly to George
ℹ West Cape Tourism Board, Corner of Castle and Burg streets ☎ 021-426 5639; www.capetourism.org
🕐 Daily 8–6

Knysna
ℹ 40 Main Street ☎ 044-382 5510; www.knysna-info.co.za 🕐 Mon–Fri 8am–5pm, Sat 8:30am–1pm

Plettenberg Bay
ℹ Shop 35, Melville Cnr ☎ 044-533 4065; www.plettenbergbay.co.za 🕐 Daily Mon–Fri 9–5, Sat–Sun 9–1

5 Greater St Lucia Wetland Park

www.sanparks.org

Running along the Indian Ocean coastline for more than 200km (120 miles) on the Mozambique border, the newly named iSimangaliso Wetland Park is among the most biodiverse of African conservation areas.

The park's wildlife checklist includes 129 species of marine and terrestrial mammal, and some 525 species of bird. The centrepiece is Lake St Lucia, Africa's largest estuarine system, separated from the ocean by a narrow silver of tall forested dunes and home to South Africa's largest concentrations of hippo and crocodile. The well-organised village of St Lucia, idyllically located in lush coastal woodland at the estuary mouth near the park's southern border, is the obvious base for exploration.

St Lucia is one of the country's top birdwatching sites, with a wide variety of aquatic species (including pelican and flamingo) living alongside garish turacos, cacophonous giant hornbills and a number of native species. It is less worthwhile for large mammals, though this is gradually changing as a result of an extensive programme of reintroductions. For now, antelope and other ungulates are well represented throughout, with the localized nyala antelope and hippo being particularly conspicuous, while the uMkhuze sector of the park also harbours significant populations of rhino and elephant. St Lucia village is also a popular

base for visits to Hluhluwe-Imfolozi (▶ 122), a superb
Big Five reserve about 45 minutes' drive inland.

Whales and dolphins are occasionally seen from the
shore, though close encounters are more likely on the
whale-watching boat trips that leave daily from St
Lucia village, weather permitting. The reefs north of
Sodwana Bay (a popular fishing resort halfway
between Kosi Bay and St Lucia village) offer some
excellent offshore snorkelling and
boat-based diving possibilities. The pristine
beaches around Rocktail Bay form the region's
most important breeding site for the endangered
leatherback and loggerhead turtles, and lodges in the
area can arrange nocturnal excursions to view nesting
turtles during the breeding season
(October–February).

✚ 24H ✉ Northeast coast of KwaZulu-Natal, running to the
Mozambican border ☎ 033-845 1000 (information)
www.kznwildlife.com (accommodation and facilities within the
park); www.elephantcoast.kzn.org.za (accommodation and
facilities outside the park) 🕐 Gates dusk to dawn
🖐 Moderate–Expensive

6 Kruger National Park

www.sanparks.org

The Kruger National Park is one of the oldest and most famous game reserves in the world, with an astonishing variety of flora and fauna.

The Kruger National Park overwhelms with its sheer size. Stretching 350km (217 miles) from the Limpopo River in the north to the Sabie River in the south, and on average 60km (37 miles) wide, the park covers nearly 2,000,000ha (5,000,000 acres).

The names of two men especially are inextricably linked with the creation of the park. The president of the old Transvaal Republic, Paul Kruger, had an area on the Sabie River declared a government reserve in 1898. During his 44 years in charge, Major James Stevenson-Hamilton, a dedicated conservationist, warded off poachers, mining companies and farmers in search of grazing from the park. He tirelessly extended the territory of the reserve, and it was under his guidance that the area was declared the Kruger National Park in 1926.

Today the park is made up of three distinct habitats: The southern region around the ever-popular Skukuza, with deciduous trees and tall grasses; the central region, mainly open savannah; and miles of *mopane* scrub in the north around Shingwedzi and Punda Maria.

Visitors must stay on the paved main roads and gravel secondary roads, but these give access to only a fraction of the park's total area. Although the Kruger is home to nearly 150 types of mammal,

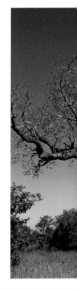

over 100 species of reptile and more than 500 species of bird, everyone wants to see the Big Five: lion, buffalo, elephant, rhino and leopard.

There are several essential dos and don'ts. Never disturb the animals. Never get out of your vehicle, except at designated viewpoints; even here you do so at your own risk. When stopping to look at potentially dangerous animals, always stop beyond them and look back – it's easier to get away in forward gear than in reverse.

✚ 23L ✉ Mpumalanga and Limpopo Province ☎ 012-428 9111 🕐 Daily, daylight hours ✋ Day admission moderate; accommodation from inexpensive to very expensive (reserve well in advance) 🍴 Restaurant, café, shop in all main camps (£) ✈ Fly to Johannesburg; flights into Skukuza available ❓ Book for walking trails one year in advance; night drives and day trails available from most camps

7 Namakwa Flowers

In springtime the arid west coast of South Africa explodes into yellow, white and purple as the year's new wild flowers appear.

South Africa's west coast from north of Cape Town all the way to Springbok in Namakwa (also spelt Namaqua) is harsh, bone-dry territory. Yet from mid-August to mid-September most years an astonishing phenomenon occurs. If the winter rains have been sufficiently heavy, and the spring is not too hot, the landscape comes alive with millions of yellow, white and purple flowers.

You don't have to go far off the beaten track to see the flowers. The **Postberg Nature Reserve** (open only during the flower season), little more than an hour's drive north of Cape Town, offers excellent viewing opportunities. An added attraction here are the wild animals: zebra, ostrich, jackal and around ten species of antelope.

However, the most spectacular displays of flowers are to be found further north, in the region around Nieuwoudtville, Kamieskroon and Springbok. Though a saloon or sedan car is perfectly adequate for a flower tour, a number of 4x4 trails have opened recently in the Namakwa and Richtersveld National Parks, giving access to the remoter parts of this thinly inhabited thirstland.

Flowers include the scarlet, yellow, purple and white blossoms of the ubiquitous succulents (mesembryanthemums), several varieties of lily, aloes and field after field of Namakwa daisies.

✚ 2D ✉ From Saldanha Bay, Western Cape, north to Springbok, Northern Cape ☎ Flower Line 027-718 2985/6 ✈ Fly to Cape Town or Springbok
ℹ Namakwa Tourism Information ☎ 027-712 8035
Postberg Nature Reserve
☎ 022-772 2144 🖐 Moderate

8 Robben Island

www.robben-island.org.za

Half an hour by boat from Cape Town harbour lies historic Robben Island, where Nelson Mandela was imprisoned.

Recently recognized as a World Heritage Site, Robben Island consists of a bleak 574ha (1,418 acres) of low-lying, wind-swept scrub. What draws hundreds of thousands of tourists here each year is not its scenic beauty but the rich history of the island and the magnificent views it affords of the Cape Peninsula.

Robben (Dutch for 'seals') Island has served as a place of confinement for society's outcasts ever since the coming of European settlers. As early as the 17th century Jan van Riebeeck banished a local rebel, Autshumato, to the island. Prominent Xhosa and Islamic leaders followed in later centuries. In the mid-19th century, Robben Island became an asylum for mental patients and then a leper colony.

But it was as a jail for apartheid's political prisoners after 1963 that Robben Island achieved its greatest notoriety. Inmates of 'The Island' included Robert Sobukwe (leader of the Pan-Africanist Congress) and several ANC leaders who would go on to serve in South Africa's first democratically elected government in 1994 – most famously Nelson Mandela who was detained here from 1964 until 1982.

Robben Island is a restricted area, which you can visit only as part of an official tour. Starting by boat from Cape Town's Waterfront (➤ 54–55), you land at Murray's Harbour. Highlights are the visit to the prison and Mandela's cell; the viewpoint from which you can see a fine panorama of the Cape Peninsula; and the island's colony of African penguins.

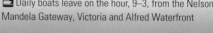

✚ 2B ✉ 11km (7 miles) off coast of Cape Town, Western Cape ☎ 021-413-4200 (Tour Line) ✋ Expensive
🚢 Daily boats leave on the hour, 9–3, from the Nelson Mandela Gateway, Victoria and Alfred Waterfront

9 uKhahlamba-Drakensburg

The green uKhahlamba-Drakensberg Mountains provide a haven for hikers, pony trekkers, trout fishermen and nature lovers.

Known to the Zulu as uKhahlamba ('Barrier of Spears') but named the Drakensberg ('Dragon's Mountains') by Dutch settlers, this cloud-scraping range stretches for hundreds of kilometres along the border between KwaZulu-Natal and Lesotho. The popular Central uKhahlamba-Drakensberg has the highest peaks, notably Injisuthi (3,410m/ 11,185ft), Champagne Castle (3,376m/11,073ft) and Giant's Castle (3,314m/10,869ft). Other popular destinations are the broad sweep of the Amphitheatre and Mont-aux-Sources in the north, and the more southerly Sani Pass into Lesotho.

The Berg, as it is locally known, with its green slopes and cold mountain streams, provides a haven for KwaZulu-Natalians escaping the heat and humidity of the subtropical east coast. An area of 2,500 sq km (956sq miles) is protected in a series of nature reserves known collectively as the uKhahlamba-Drakensberg Park, which was designated a World Heritage Site in 2000. The park is managed by the provincial parks board Ezemvelo KwaZulu-Natal Wildlife (EKZNW), which offers camping facilities and accommodation in serviced chalets. You can watch bearded vultures feeding at Giant's Castle, or go trout fishing at Kamberg.

In earlier centuries, the indigenous community took refuge in the uKhahlamba-Drakensberg when

they were driven from the lower-lying areas by European settlers and African tribes. Beautiful rock paintings by the native inhabtants can be seen on more than 500 caves and rock shelters studded across the park.

Some of South Africa's best walking and hiking can be found in these mountains, including gentle strolls through the foothills.

✚ 11E ✉ Western KwaZulu-Natal, along the border with Lesotho ☎ 033-845 1000 (information); to reserve, www.kznwildlife.com 🕓 The various nature reserves are usually open during daylight hours ✋ Moderate

10 Victoria and Alfred Waterfront

www.waterfront.co.za

A complex of shops, cinemas, museums, restaurants and hotels makes up Cape Town's ever-popular Victoria and Alfred Waterfront.

Since the early 1990s, a handful of rundown buildings in Cape Town harbour have metamorphosed into one of the country's premier tourist attractions, the Victoria and Alfred Waterfront. Several factors contribute to its success: the architecture and the superb views, but perhaps most important of all, the peculiar charm of the combination of genuine working harbour and leisure spot.

The Waterfront offers a wide spectrum of entertainment – a choice of cinemas, one with a five-storey-high IMAX screen, a theatre, a sports café, nightclubs, and music venues, the best-known being the Green Dolphin for jazz. In summer you can enjoy street performers and live music in the outdoor amphitheatre. The complex also has dozens of eating places, ranging from fast-food outlets, to steakhouses, pizzerias, seafood bars and expensive restaurants. The most atmospheric of the pubs is Ferryman's Tavern, housed in a converted warehouse.

Although prices in the shops here seem expensive to locals, they are reasonable if you are spending US dollars, pounds sterling or euros. Outlets offer books, clothing of all sorts, fine foods and wines, electrical goods, gifts, local art and curios. There are also several indoor craft markets.

Other places of interest at the Waterfront include the South African Maritime Museum, the floating Victoria Museum Ship, the Two Oceans Aquarium (► 88), and the platform next to Bertie's Landing where Cape fur seals bask. Various tours are available from here, too: a sunset cruise in Table Bay, helicopter flights over the Peninsula, and trips around and to Robben Island (► 50–51).

✚ *Cape Town 6b* ✉ Dock Road, Cape Town, Western Cape ☎ 021-408 7600 (information) 🕐 Restaurants, pubs open daily until late; shops open daily 9–9 💰 Free 🍴 Huge variety to choose from 🚌 Buses from Cape Town Station and Sea Point ❓ Phone for details of live events

Best things to do

Good places to have lunch

Café Riche (£–££)
Oldest café in Pretoria, and very centrally located for people-watching. A good selection of light lunches.
✉ 2 Church Square, Pretoria, Gauteng ☎ 012-328 3173

Charlie Croft's Dockside Diner (££)
Named after the port engineer whop dredged Durban harbour in 1890, this place serves great seafood complimented by a good wine list and great harbour views.
✉ Wilson's Wharf, Victoria Embankment, Durban, ZwaZulu-Natal
☎ 031-307 2935

Coachman's Inn (££)
Set in a mock Tudor building. Wide-ranging international food with strong French influence. The restaurant has maintained a consistently good quality over more than 25 years.
✉ 29 Peter Place, Lyme Park, Sandton, Johannesburg, Gauteng
☎ 011-706 7269

Cock House (££)
Restaurant and guest house in a homestead built in 1826, a former residence of the novelist Andre Brink and now a national monument.
✉ 10 Market Street, Grahamstown, Eastern Cape ☎ 046-636 1287

Hippo Hollow Country Estate (£–£££)
Stylish décor, good food and a superb wine list complement the bush setting overlooking the Sabi River, home to hippos, crocs and a profusion of birds. A convenient lunch break en route to the Kruger National Park.
✉ R40, Hazyview, Mpumalanga ☎ 013-737 7752; www,hippohollow.co.za

Kapitan's Café (££)
This idiosyncratically decorated Indian eatery in downtown

Johannesburg, soon to celebrate its centenary, was a favoured lunchtime haunt of Nelson Mandela in the 1950s. The curries remain superb.

✉ 11a Kort Street, Johannesburg, Gauteng
☎ 011-834 8048

Mount Nelson (£££)

Famous luxury hotel with three fine restaurants, most prestigiously the elegantly designed Cape Colony.

✉ 76 Orange Street, Cape Town, Western Cape ☎ 021-483 1000

Sani Top Chalet (£–££)

Africa's highest pub. Hearty fare accompanied by the stunning view from the chilly summit of the only road crossing the 200km (124 miles) border between KwaZulu-Natal and Lesotho.

✉ Sani Pass, near Himeville, ZwaZulu-Natal ☎ 033-792 1305; www.sanitopchalet.co.za

The Wild Fig (££)

Housed in an 18th-century barn, this restaurant offers a blend of Thai, South African and Greek specialties –great cripsy duck.

✉ Courtyard Hotel complex, Liesbeeck Avenue, Mowbray, Cape Town, Western Cape ☎ 021-448 0507

Vineyard Hotel (££–£££)

A choice of restaurants, including The Square, a brasserie style eatery and sushi bar. Superb views from the large garden.

✉ Colinton Road, Newlands, Cape Town, Western Cape ☎ 021-683 3044

Great beaches

Bloubergstrand, Cape Town
Mainly for the much photographed view across Table Bay to Table Mountain – good windsurfing too, though the water is cold in winter.

Clifton, Cape Town
Very fashionable sunbathing spot, with dazzlingly white sands.

Muizenberg, Cape Town
Popular swimming and surfing beach.

Plettenberg Bay, Garden Route
Some of the best golden, sandy beaches in South Africa (➤ 42).

Nature's Valley, Garden Route
Beautiful stretch of golden sand hemmed in by pristine hardwood forests (➤ 43).

Jeffrey's Bay, Garden Route
The country's top surfing beach attracts devotees from around the world.

Nahoon Beach, East London
Outstanding surfing beach (▶ 93).

North Beach, Durban
The most popular and populous beach in the country.

Thonga Beach, Greater St Lucia Wetland Park
Wonderfully isolated beach hemmed in by wooded dunes. Great snorkelling from the beach.

Rocktail Bay, Greater St Lucia Wetland Park
Effectively a private beach, set below wild cliffs, with no habitation for miles in any direction.

Places to take the children

Boulders Beach Penguins
This pretty beach has a colony of African penguins.
✉ Boulders Beach, south of Simon's Town, Cape Town

Golden Mile, Durban
This is paradise for children, offering beach, lawns, paddling pools, rides in boats and rickshaws, Minitown – a miniature city spread over 1.2ha (3 acres), with buildings, trains, a snake park and uShaka Marine World (➤ 112).

Gold Reef City, Johannesburg
Theme park with many rides and amusements for children (➤ 146).

Johannesburg Zoo and Zoo Lake
One of the best places in this city to take the family: bears, lions, elephants, and row boats on the lake (➤ 147).

Mini Blue Train
A miniature steam engine pulls passenger coaches along a circular small-gauge track with views out to the sea and of the lawns. Mini-golf is also available.

✉ Mouille Point, next to the lighthouse, Cape Town ☎ 021-434 8537
🕓 Mon–Fri 3–5, Sat–Sun 11–5

Margate Pleasureland
Amusement park with bumper cars, ferris wheel, water slide and a variety of other rides for children.

✉ Margate Beach, ZwaZulu-Natal ☎ (cell) 039-312 0864

Outeniqua Choo Tjoe, Garden Route
This steam train runs daily from George to Knysna. The beautifully scenic route takes in beaches, woodlands and the spectacular Kaaimans River bridge crossing. Seven-hour round trip, including a two-hour stop in Knysna.

✉ Station Street, George, Garden Route ☎ 044-801 8288

Planetarium
The University of Witwatersrand runs Saturday morning shows designed specially for children aged 5 to 8 in it's planetarium.

✉ Yale Road, Johannesburg, Gauteng ☎ 011-717 1392; www.wits.ac.za/planetarium 🕓 Sat 10:30

Ratanga Junction
South Africa's biggest theme park offers roller-coasters, water rides, live entertainment, restaurants and cinemas.

✉ Off the N1, Sable Road, Cape Town, Western Cape ☎ 086-120 0300; www.ratanga.co.za 🕓 Dec–Apr, Wed–Sun 10–5

Two Oceans Aquarium
Has a section where children can handle shells and sea creatures (► 88).

Best nature reserves

Addo Elephant National Park
The most intimate elephant watching in South Africa. Good for rhino too (➤ 92).

Augrabies Falls National Park
The gorge carved by this spectacular waterfall on the Gariep River bisects a thrillingly barren lunar rockscape studded with weird succulents (➤ 172).

Blyde River Canyon Nature Reserve
Stunning viewpoints and intimate forest footpaths on the Mpumalanga escarpment (➤ 36–37).

Golden Gate Highlands National Park
The Free State's top attraction, set in part of the Drakensberg foothills known for its wildlife and sandstone formations (➤ 175).

Greater St Lucia Wetland Park
Protects a vast complex of coastal wetlands supporting more than 500 bird species and large concentrations of hippo and crocodile (➤ 44–45).

Hluhluwe-Imfolozi National Park
Big Five reserve known in particular for great rhinoceros-viewing (➤ 122).

Kgalagadi Transfrontier Park
This desiccated sea of red dunes is home to the gemsbok and a surprising variety of carnivores and raptors (➤ 176).

Kruger National Park
One of Africa's truly great reserves, an unimaginably vast tract of bush known for its great Big Five sightings and much more (➤ 46–47).

Stunning views

The Amphitheatre, Royal Natal Park, uKhahlamba-Drakensberg
(➤ 52–53).

Three Rondawels Viewpoint, Blyde River Nature Reserve
(➤ 36–37).

Olifants Camp, on a cliff overlooking the Olifants River, Kruger
National Park (➤ 46–47).

Robberg Nature Reserve, Plettenberg Bay, Garden Route
(➤ 42–43).

Cape Point, Cape Peninsula (➤ 38–39).

Franschhoek Valley, Cape Winelands.

Storms River Mouth, Tsitsikama National Park (➤ 43).

Augrabies Falls, Northern Cape (➤ 172).

Hole in the Wall rock formation, Wild Coast.

a walk
around historic Cape Town

This walk takes you right through the heart of the old city.

Start from the Grand Parade, between the Castle (▶ 78–79) and the City Hall.

The ornate 1905 City Hall overlooks the Grand Parade, where 100,000 people came to hear Nelson Mandela speak on his release from prison.

Walk along Strand Street and turn left onto Adderley Street.

Walking along Adderley, Cape Town's main street, you will see on your left flower stalls, the grand 19th-century Standard Bank, the Groote Kerk (▶ 81) and the Slave Lodge (▶ 85).

Continue on straight up Government Avenue pedestrian way.

To your left is the back of Parliament and the stately Tuynhuys, now the State President's office. If you detour a little to your right you will find yourself in the heart of the Company's Garden (▶ 79).

Turn right across the front of the South African Museum (▶ 86–87), left up Grey's Pass, right into Orange, and then right again into Long Street (▶ 82–83).

If you are feeling tired you can relax at the baths here. Otherwise go window shopping or enjoy a drink at one of the many cafés.

Go down Long Street, turn right into Church Street, then left into Burg, right into Longmarket, down the side of Greenmarket Square (➤ 81), and then left along the pedestrian precinct of St George's Mall.

This is the heart of commercial Cape Town. In summer the area is alive with street performers, traders and shoppers.

Turn right into Strand, which will take you back to the Grand Parade.

Distance 3km (2 miles)
Time 1 hour without stops, 3 hours with stops
Start/end point Grand Parade ✚ *Cape Town 6e*
Tea or lunch Tea room in Company's Garden (£) ✉ Off Government Avenue ☎ 021-400 2521

Top sporting events

2010 FIFA World Cup

Expect the football-crazed media and public to crank into overdrive during the build up to 2010, when the world's premier sporting event is hosted on South African soil.
www.fifa.com; **www**.worldcup2010southafrica.com

International rugby

Whether it's a national test or a fixture on the Super 14 competition, which pits South Africa's top five franchises against their New Zealand and Australian counterparts, few sports generate as much passion among South African spectators as rugby.
www.sarugby.net

Cape Argus Cycle Tour

South Africa's most prestigious and scenic on-road cycling event, covering the Cape Peninsula, is now 30 years old and still going strong.
www.cycletour.co.za

Comrades Marathon

South Africa's most gruelling marathon, normally held in June, runs between Durban and Pietermaritzburg, alternating annually between 'down' and 'up' directions (2007 being a down run from Pietermaritzburg to Durban).

www.comrades.com

Nedbank Golf Challenge

The most popular tournament on the local golfing calendar, with a field of top class international golfers batting for honours at the country's top golf course, the Gary Player Country Club at Sun City.

www.nedbankgolfchallenge.com

International cricket

The world's top ranked one day international side at the time of writing, the Proteas' home season runs from September to March, with a reliable highlight being the five-day 'New Year' test at Cape Town's spectacular Newlands, in the shadow of Table Mountain.

www.cricinfo.com

Horse racing

Check any newspaper for upcoming events, but the one to be seen at is the Durban July, the South African equivalent of the Royal Ascot.

www.durbanjuly.info

Two Oceans Marathon

This 56km (35 mile) marathon, held over the Easter weekend, crosses the scenic Cape Peninsula.

www.twooceansmarathon.org.za

Exploring

South Africa is remarkably diverse. It's difficult to even begin to do it justice in the space of a vacation. There's Cape Town, regarded by many to be the world's most beautiful city, its pervasive sense of history complemented by a seemingly endless string of postcard-perfect beaches and spectacular mountains. There's the Kruger Park, a game reserve as large as Wales, home to a prodigious Aardvark-to-Zebra of wildlife – lion, leopard, rhino, elephant, giraffe, you name it – and the even bigger Kgalagadi Transfrontier Park in the remote Kalahari Desert on the Botswana border. There are seven World Heritage Sites, ranging from the lofty peaks of the uKhahlamba-Drakensberg to the mysterious medieval stone ruins of Mapungubwe, not to mention a coastline that extends over 3,000km and offers swimming, water sports and sunbathing. South Africa really does have something for everybody.

Western and Eastern Capes

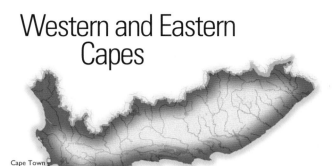

Cape Town

The Western and Eastern Capes offer the visitor a full and varied selection of forested mountains, endless beaches, sun-baked plains not to mention several historical towns and the unforgettable Cape Town.

Unlike the rest of South Africa, the Western Cape has a Mediterranean climate, with mild, wet winters and hot, dry summers. As this region was the earliest to be occupied by European settlers, some of the oldest towns and buildings in the country are here. Visitors come to enjoy the sheer natural beauty

of the Cape, tour its vineyards, soak up the atmosphere of its towns and relax on its beaches.

The scenic Garden Route provides a gateway from the Western into the Eastern Cape, a region steeped in a history of contact and conflict between the Xhosa people and European settlers. Grahamstown will fascinate those interested in the past, while nature-lovers will want to head for the Addo Elephant National Park and the vast empty beaches of the Wild Coast.

CAPE TOWN

Cape Town's varied history and combination of mountains and sea make it one of the most attractive cities in the world. Known affectionately as the Mother City, it is by far the oldest urban centre in South Africa. In 1652 the Dutch East India Company sent Jan van Riebeeck here to establish a fresh-produce garden (the Company's Garden, ➤ 79) to supply its passing ships. The small way station grew gradually into a town, then into a city, passing from Dutch to British control in 1795. After the formation of the Union in 1910, Cape Town became, and remains, the legislative capital of the country and seat of Parliament.

Present-day Cape Town is a cosmopolitan place, populated by a mix of peoples descended from the indigenous Khoi, slaves originally brought here from Indonesia, Angola, Madagascar and Mozambique, settlers from many countries of Europe and, increasingly, Xhosa-speaking people from the Eastern Cape.

Superbly situated at the foot of Table Mountain, the city offers many things to do and see: mountain walks, swimming from beautiful beaches, scenic drives, museums, art galleries, historic monuments and many restaurants and music venues. Once you have exhausted the pleasures of Cape Town, there is plenty to enjoy in the surrounding region. Within a day's drive of the city you

can sample wines at the farms along the Wine Route, watch whales at Hermanus (➤ 96), see the spring flowers to the north (➤ 48–49), and visit beautiful towns such as Stellenbosch and Tulbagh (➤ 101, 102). ✚ 2A ✉ Western Cape

Bertram House

This Georgian redbrick house was built by an English attorney, John Barker, in the 1830s. It is now an off-shoot of the Slave Lodge (➤ 85) and houses a collection of fine furniture, *objets d'art*, silver and ceramics. The house and its contents give a good insight of what everyday life was like for a well-to-do English family at the Cape in the 19th century.

✚ *Cape Town 5f* ✉ Corner of Government Avenue and Orange Street
☎ 021-481 3940 ⏰ Tue–Thu 10–4. Closed public holidays ✋ Inexpensive
🍴 Café (££)

Bo-Kaap

The Bo-Kaap (Upper-Cape) or Malay Quarter lies on the steep slopes of Signal Hill, directly above the city. In the 19th century it became, and remains today, a predominantly Muslim area. At the **Bo-Kaap Museum** you will get a vivid impression of the life of the Muslim community and its contribution to the making of the Afrikaans language and to Cape culture. Walking tours of the picturesque cobbled streets and brightly painted terraced cottages of the Bo-Kaap start from the museum.

➕ *Cape Town 5d*

Bo-Kaap Museum

✉ 71 Wale Street ☎ 021-481 3939; www.iziko.org.za ⏰ Mon–Sat 9–4:30 💷 Inexpensive

Cape Peninsula and Table Mountain

Best places to see, ➤ 38–39.

Castle of Good Hope

The pentagonal layout and five angled bastions of the Castle of Good Hope were the latest in military architecture when it was begun in 1666. Completed in 1679, the Castle is the oldest European building in South Africa. The central courtyard gives access to the beautiful Kat Balcony of 1785, by Anton Anreith, one of the Cape's most famous sculptors. Don't miss the William Fehr Collection of art.

The paintings give a fascinating series of views of the changing appearance of Cape Town, from the 17th to the 20th centuries.

🞢 *Cape Town 7e* ✉ Buitenkant Street ☎ 021-464 1260 🕓 Daily 9:30–4 👋 Moderate 🍴 Café (£) ❓ Phone for details of guided tours, open days

Company's Garden

The garden Jan van Riebeeck established for the Dutch East India Company in the 17th century is still in place – though lawns, roses and indigenous trees grow there now rather than the original fruit and vegetables. Tree-shaded Government Avenue runs the whole length of the garden, giving access to its museums and galleries. Situated in the heart of the city, it is a place where you can relax, feed the squirrels and pigeons, and enjoy a drink or a light meal at the open-air restaurant.

🞢 *Cape Town 5f* ✉ Government Avenue 🕓 7–sunset 👋 Free 🍴 Tea room (£)

District Six Museum

District Six was the site of a vibrant working-class community which was destroyed by the apartheid laws in the 1960s and '70s. The inhabitants of the area were forcibly removed and their houses bulldozed to make way for a white suburb. Such was the opposition to this action that most of the land has since remained unoccupied. The District Six Museum commemorates this episode with a wealth of photographs and other documentation.
www.districtsix.co.za

✚ *Cape Town 6f* ✉ 25A Buitenkant Street ☎ 021-446 7200 🕐 Mon 9–2:30, Tue–Sat 9–4 ✋ Inexpensive

Greenmarket Square

Laid out as a fresh produce market in 1710, today this pleasant square houses a flea market (Mon–Sat 9–4). Weather permitting, you can bargain here for jewellery, crafts, artworks, curios and clothing. The 18th-century Old Town House on the southwest side of the square was formerly a town hall and now houses the outstanding **Michaelis Collection** of early Dutch and Flemish painting.

✚ *Cape Town 6e*

Michaelis Collection

✉ Corner of Longmarket and Burg streets ☎ 021-481 3933 🕐 Mon–Fri 10–5, Sat 10–4 ✋ Inexpensive

Groote Kerk

The origins of the Groote Kerk (Big Church), the mother church of the Dutch Reformed Church in South Africa, go back to 1704. This simple thatched structure was replaced in 1841 by the present church; only the old clock tower remains. One of the most striking features is the church's fine wooden pulpit.

✚ *Cape Town 6e* ✉ 39 Adderley Street ☎ 021-461 7044 🕐 Mon–Fri 10–2 ✋ Free ❓ Guided tours

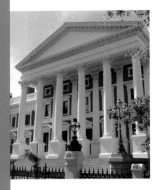

Houses of Parliament

Dating back to 1884, the Houses of Parliament have been modified several times to accommodate successive political dispensations. Today they house the legislature of the fully representative government first elected in 1994. Sessions of parliament are open to the public during the first half of the year; in the second half, guided tours are available of the buildings and their gallery of historical paintings and parliamentary memorabilia.

🚹 *Cape Town 6e* ✉ Parliament Street ☎ 021-403 2911 🕒 Open daily 🖐 Free ❓ Hourly guided tours on weekdays; phone for details

Long Street

Aptly named Long Street runs the whole length of Cape Town, from sea to mountain. Alternately seedy and striking, the street is becoming increasingly the home of agents and lodges catering to budget travellers. There are also churches, a mosque, second-hand bookshops, louche all-night bars, clubs and cafés, tattoo parlours, sex shops and junk emporia. Long Street is a wonderful gallery of late Victorian commercial architecture displaying many interesting details in plaster, wrought iron, ceramic and stonework. The interior of the **Long Street Baths,** at the head of the street, is in classic Edwardian style, and you can have a swim, Turkish bath or massage here.

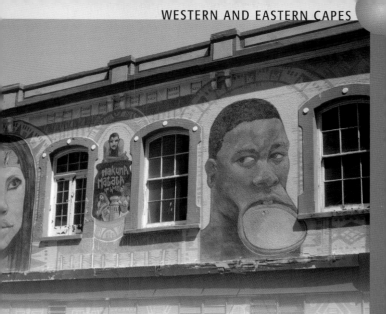

✚ *Cape Town 5e–6d*
Long Street Baths
☎ 021-400 3302 🕐 Swimming, men and women: Mon–Sat 7am–8pm, Sun 8–7 (Tue 10–4 women only) 👐 Inexpensive to moderate ❓ Steam baths and massage available, phone for details

Lutheran Church and Parsonage
The ubiquitous Anton Anreith had a hand in both these buildings, as carver of the striking wooden pulpit in the Lutheran Church and as architect of the adjoining parsonage. The church was built by the wealthy merchant, Martin Melck, in 1774, shortly after freedom of worship was granted to the Lutherans at the Cape. The handsome building next door, now in use as offices, was originally the parsonage.
✚ *Cape Town 6d* ✉ 19 Buitengracht Street ☎ 021-421 5854 🕐 Mon, Wed, Fri 10–2 👐 Free

Rust en Vreugd

The William Fehr Collection of art relating to South Africa is divided between the Castle of Good Hope (➤ 78–79) and Rust en Vreugd (Rest and Joy). But it is not only the display of furniture, paintings, and watercolours by Thomas Baines that is worth seeing here. The house itself, with its beautiful proportions and handsome pillared porch, is one of the best examples of 18th-century domestic architecture in Cape Town. The formal garden is modelled on Cape Dutch gardens of the period.
www.iziko.org.za

✚ *Cape Town 6f* ✉ 78 Buitenkant Street
☎ 021-464 3280 🕐 Mon–Fri 8:30–4:30
✋ Entrance by donation

St George's Catherdral

The present Anglican cathedral, designed by architect Sir Herbert Baker, was completed in 1901, replacing the original building of 1834. The grey neo-Gothic edifice is more impressive inside than outside. Particularly striking are the modern stained-glass windows depicting the Creation, and the 8m (26ft) rose window by Francis Spear. The window above the transept is dedicated to the British admiral and statesman Lord Louis Mountbatten.

St George's most famous incumbent was Archbishop Desmond Tutu who retired in 1996.

www.stgeorgecathedral.com

✚ *Cape Town 6e* ✉ 5 Wale Street ☎ 021-424 7360 ⏰ Mon–Fri 6:30–6, Sat 7–noon, Sun 6:30–noon 🖐 Free

Slave Lodge

First built in 1685, this handsome white building has had a varied history as a slave lodge, brothel and Supreme Court, and is now a museum of cultural history. The collection includes not only extensive materials illustrating the cultures of the different communities in South Africa, but also objects from elsewhere in the world. Parts of the collection are displayed at Bertram House (➤ 77) and the Bo-Kaap Museum (➤ 78).

www.iziko.org.za

✚ *Cape Town 6e* ✉ 49 Adderley Street ☎ 021-460 8240 ⏰ Mon–Fri 8:30–4:30, Sat 8:30–1 🖐 Inexpensive

South African Library

Founded in 1818, this was one of the earliest free libraries in
the world. A donation of books provided its first stock, and it
was maintained till 1829 by a tax on wine. One of its greatest
treasures is the collection of 5,000 volumes given by Sir George
Grey, a former governor of the Cape, which includes illuminated
medieval manuscripts. Exhibitions from the collection are held
regularly in the library.

✚ *Cape Town 5e* ✉ 5 Queen Victoria Street ☎ 021-424 6320
🕐 Mon–Fri 2–5 ✋ Free

South African Museum and Planetarium

This museum, the oldest on the subcontinent, was opened in
1825, and moved to its present building in 1897; it was originally

housed in what is now the Slave Lodge (► 85). The main emphases here are on the anthropology, implements and art of Southern Africa's earliest inhabitants, as well as natural history, animals, fossils and geology. You can listen to recorded whale sounds in the ever-popular Whale Hall, while viewing the skeletons of a variety of these huge mammals hanging from the ceiling. The adjoining Planetarium offers regularly changing shows of the Southern hemisphere's night skies and evening lectures.

www.iziko.org.za

✚ *Cape Town 5f* ✉ 25 Queen Victoria Street ☎ 021-481 3800 ⚙ Museum 10–5 ✋ Inexpensive; Sun free 🍴 Café (££) ❓ Phone for details of Planetarium shows ☎ 021-481 3900

South African National Gallery

In former years this gallery displayed mainly European art, and its

earlier collection included paintings by 17th-century Italian masters and works by Stubbs and Victorian painters. But more recently the gallery has concentrated on South African art: international-style paintings and sculpture, photography, so-called 'township art' and traditional art-forms such as beadwork. The gallery regularly holds temporary exhibitions.

✚ *Cape Town 5f* ✉ Government Avenue, Company's Garden ☎ 021-467 4660 ⚙ Tue–Sun 10–5. Closed 1 May ✋ Inexpensive 🍴 Café (££)

Table Mountain Cableway

Table Mountain towers dramatically 1,086m (3,562ft) above Cape Town. A good stiff walk will get you to the top and back again in about five hours. The recently upgraded cableway takes the less energetic to the top in five minutes, with the large cable-cars revolving through 360 degrees to give a panoramic outlook. Visitors can ramble over the almost flat 'tabletop' to enjoy the fabulous views which open up in every direction. In summer look for the spectacular 'tablecloth' of cloud which often spreads over the mountain. See Best places to see ➤ 38–39.

www.tablemountain.net

✚ *Cape Town 4f (off map)* ✉ Tafelberg Road ☎ 021-424 8181
🕓 Generally daylight hours; Dec–Jan 7:30am–10pm; phone for seasonal variations 🖐 Expensive 🍴 Restaurant and café (££)

Two Oceans Aquarium

This beautiful aquarium concentrates on marine life from the two oceans that some claim (somewhat arbitrarily) meet at Cape Point: the Indian and the Atlantic. Its tanks display commercial fish such as yellowtail and snoek, and brilliantly hued tropical species, as well as sharks, moray eels, penguins and seals. A highlight is the kelp forest waving hypnotically to and fro in a huge tank, nearly 10m (33ft) high. Upstairs is a tank where children can touch various species.

www.aquarium.co.za

✚ *Cape Town 5b* ✉ Dock Road, Victoria and Alfred Waterfront
☎ 021-418 3823 🕓 Daily 9:30–6 🖐 Expensive 🍴 Restaurant (££)
☎ 021-419 9068

Victoria and Alfred Waterfront

Best places to see, ➤ 54–55.

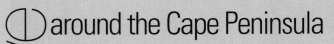

around the Cape Peninsula

The most scenic parts of the Cape Peninsula can be seen on this drive.

Take the M3 out of the city (signed Muizenberg).

You will pass Groote Schuur Hospital (left), site of the world's first heart transplant, before climbing over Wynberg Hill and down into the Constantia Valley.

The M3 ends at a T-junction. Turn left on to the M42, then right at the next T-junction on to the Main Road (M4) which skirts Muizenberg and then winds along the False Bay coast through Fish Hoek to Simon's Town.

Muizenberg and Fish Hoek have excellent swimming beaches. Simon's Town is worth visiting for its delightful Victorian shopfronts and pleasant waterfront.

Going south from Simon's Town on the M4 you soon reach the left-hand turn-off to The Boulders.

The Boulders, a pretty beach among huge granite boulders, is home to an African penguin colony.

Continue south on the M4 until the road climbs away from the sea, becoming the M65, and reaches the left-hand turn-off to the Cape of Good Hope sector of Table Mountain National Park.

If you have the time, detour south through the park to Cape Point; you may see some wildlife on the way, and the restaurant offers stunning views over False Bay.

Keep following the M65 across the peninsula. Skirting

*the Atlantic coast via Scarborough and Kommetjie you
reach Sun Valley. Turn left here and follow the M64
(Ou Kaapse Weg, 'Old Cape Road') over the mountain.*

At the highest point of the Ou Kaapse Weg you will see the
entrance (left) to the former Silvermine Nature Reserve,
which now forms part of Table Mountain National Park.
There are easy walking paths around the picturesque dam.

*When the Ou Kaapse Weg ends at a T-junction turn left
on to the M42 and continue until the M41. Turn left here,
the winding road that climbs up to Constantia Nek.*

Soon after turning on to the M42, pass Pollsmoor Prison
(right) where Nelson Mandela spent several years. Drive
through Tokai Forest and the vineyards of Constantia. On
the M41 is the turn-off to Groot Constantia (➤ 95).

From Constantia Nek descend via the M63 to Hout Bay.

Stop at Hout Bay for seafood at Mariner's Wharf. There are
boat trips from here to nearby Duiker Island, where you
can see Cape fur seals, bank cormorants, Cape
cormorants, Cape gannets, kelp gulls and arctic skuas.

*From Hout Bay, take the M6 along the coast. Just past
Camps Bay turn right off the M6 on to Lower Kloof
Road, then very soon sharp right on to Kloof Road. This
takes you through the 'Glen' up to Kloof Nek. From there
descend via Kloof Nek Road back down to the city.*

Distance 110km (68 miles)
Time 3 hours (depending on traffic) without stops, 6 hours with stops
Start/end point Cape Town city centre ✚ 27T
Lunch Bulsfontein Visitors Centre & Two Oceans Restaurant (£–££)
✉ Cape of Good Hope ☎ 021-780 9204

More to see in the Western and Eastern Capes

ADDO ELEPHANT NATIONAL PARK

The relict elephant population that inhabits the dense scrub of Addo (from the Khoikhoi 'Gadouw,' meaning river crossing) had been hunted close to extinction when this area of 100,000ha (250,000 acres) was proclaimed a national park in 1931. Today, the vastly expanded park supports around 500 elephants, and ranks as one of the most biodiverse in Africa, running from the Indian Ocean coastline to the barren and mountainous Little Karoo. Addo is renowned for its very relaxed (but not, as is widely claimed, especially short-tusked) elephants, but other wildlife includes black rhino, buffalo, eland, red hartebeest, kudu and bushbuck, while lion and spotted hyena were reintroduced in 2003. Take care not to run over one of the park's smallest inhabitants, the flightless dung beetle, which is most often seen after rain, rolling away a rounded dung ball for use as food and a hatchery for its eggs. Two walking trails can be reserved in the park.

www.sanparks.org

✚ 7B ✉ Eastern Cape ☎ 012-428 9111 ✋ Moderate

EAST LONDON

Situated on the Buffalo River, East London gained its present name in 1847; it was known previously as Port Rex. The city has two of the best surfing beaches in the country, Eastern Beach and Nahoon Beach. Its main cultural attractions are the **East London Museum** and the **Ann Bryant Art Gallery.** The former contains an extensive natural history display, including the world's only dodo egg and a stuffed coelacanth. (The first specimen of this fish, thought to have been extinct for 65 million years, was caught off East London in 1938 and brought to the museum.) The art gallery displays works by British and South African artists of the late 19th century onwards.

✚ 9B ✉ Eastern Cape

East London Museum

✉ 319 Oxford Street ☎ 043-743 0689 ⏱ Mon–Fri 9:30–5, Sat 2–5, Sun 11:30–3 ✋ Inexpensive

Ann Bryant Art Gallery

✉ 9 St Marks Road, Southern Wood ☎ 043-726 4356; www.annbryant.co.za ⏱ Mon–Fri 9–5, Sat 9:30–12 ✋ Free

GARDEN ROUTE
Best places to see, ➤ 42–43.

GRAAFF-REINET AND NIEU BETHESDA
Known as the 'gem of the Karoo', Graaff-Reinet is a treasure house of 19th-century Cape Dutch architecture. More than 200 of the town's buildings have been declared national monuments. An interesting historical museum occupies **Reinet House.**

At Nieu Bethesda, 50km (31 miles) to the north, the weird **Owl House,** home of artist Helen Martins, who committed suicide in 1976, is filled with her murals of bright ground glass and concrete sculptures of owls, camels, mermaids and nativity scenes.

www.graaffreinet.co.za

✚ 7C ✉ Eastern Cape

ℹ Graaff-Reinet Publicity Association ☎ 049-892-4248 (also fax)

Reinet House
✉ Murray Street ☎ 049-892 3801 🕐 Mon–Fri 8–12:30, 2–5, Sat 9–12 ✋ Inexpensive

Owl House
✉ Nuwe Straat (street) ☎ 049-841 1603; www.owlhouse.co.za 🕐 Daily 9–6 ✋ Inexpensive

GRAHAMSTOWN
Grahamstown, founded in 1812 as a military settlement during the ongoing wars between the British and the Xhosa, is best known for its many churches and educational institutions, and for the National Arts Festival (➤ 24). The town's most imposing building is the Cathedral of St Michael and St George, dating back to 1824. The **Albany Museum** gives a good idea of the culture of the indigenous Xhosa, and of the settlers who came here in 1820. The **Observatory Museum** houses a working camera obscura.

www.grahamstown.co.za

✚ 8B ✉ Eastern Cape

🛈 63 High Street ☎ 046-622 3241 ⏰ Mon–Fri 8:30–5; Sat 9–1
Albany Museum
✉ Somerset Street ☎ 046-622 2312 ⏰ Tue–Fri 8–1, 2–5; Sat 9–1
✋ Inexpensive
Observatory Museum
✉ Bathurst Street ☎ 046-622 2312 ⏰ Mon–Fri 9:30–1, 2–5; Sat 9–1
✋ Inexpensive

GROOT CONSTANTIA

Groot (Great) Constantia is one of the oldest wine estates in South Africa, having been granted to Governor Simon van der Stel in 1685. The Cape Dutch manor house with its collection of period furniture and silverware dates back originally to the 17th century. It was gutted by fire in 1925, but has been faithfully restored. The wine cellar was built in the late 1700s and is now a wine museum.
www.groot-constantia.co.za
➕ 27S ✉ Off the M41, Constantia, Western Cape ☎ 021-794 5128
⏰ 10–5 ✋ Inexpensive 🍴 Tavern (££); Jonkershuis (£££)

HERMANUS

This popular seaside resort offers good beaches, a busy flea market, restaurants and walks in the nearby Fernkloof Nature Reserve. But the major attraction is the southern right whales; which come annually to calve in the bay, from September to December. A 'whale crier' alerts visitors to their presence with blasts on his seaweed horn. If you're lucky you may see whales within a couple of metres of the Old Harbour wall, but binoculars are advisable. A good vantage point is the scenic path running along the cliffs.

www.hermanus.co.za

➕ 3A ✉ Western Cape

ℹ Old Station Building, Mitchell Street

☎ 028-312 2629 🕓 Mon–Fri 8–6, Sat 9–5, Sun 9–3

HOGSBACK

Hogsback is a favourite holiday resort for the city-dwellers of the Eastern Cape. Situated in the Amatola Mountains, it offers trout fishing and walks through virgin forest. At 1,200–1,300m (3,936–4,264ft) above sea level the area is cool in summer and often blanketed in snow during the winter. The Arboretum, a living museum of trees, contains many indigenous species such as yellowwoods, white ironwood and assegai-wood, as well as exotics such as California redwoods and holy cypresses.

➕ 8C ✉ Eastern Cape
ℹ️ Nina's Deli can provide tourist info and maps
☎ 045-962 1326

KIRSTENBOSCH

Set on the eastern slopes of Table Mountain, Kirstenbosch is among the world's finest botanical gardens, and contains nearly 7,000 species, of which about 900 occur naturally in the unplanted areas of the garden. In the planted areas look for the magnificent proteas, cycads, restios, succulents and aloes. The conservatory houses desert species, and don't miss the magical, crystal-clear pool, Colonel Bird's Bath, in its secluded dell. The shop sells plants, souvenirs and books. Concerts are held on the lawns on Sunday afternoons in summer, and there is a braille trail and scent garden for the blind.

www.sanbi.org

➕ 27S ✉ Rhodes Drive, Western Cape ☎ 021-799 8899
🕐 Summer 8–7; winter 8–6 ✋ Moderate 🍴 Restaurant and café (££)

MONTAGU HOT SPRINGS

The small town of Montagu, founded in 1851, is reached via a pass cut through wonderfully contorted strata of red stone. The hot springs for which the town is best known may be visited just for the day or as part of a longer stay at the adjoining hotel and chalets. While in the area visit the vineyards in the Robertson district, and the amazing cactus nursery near Ashton.

www.tourismmontagu.co.za

➕ 3B ✉ Western Cape ❓ Hot springs and Avalon Springs Hotel

🕐 Daily 8–5 ☎ 023-614 1150; www.avalonsprings.co.za

ℹ 24 Bath Street ☎ 023-614 2471

MOUNTAIN ZEBRA NATIONAL PARK

Occupying some 6,500ha (16,055 acres) of mountainous Karoo landscape near Cradock, this park was originally created to accommodate the nearly extinct Cape mountain zebra *(Equus z. zebra)*, which is distinguishable from the southern race of the

more widespread Burchell's zebra *(Equus (quagga) burchelli)* by its lack of 'shadow stripes' and small dewlap. It now supports 300 zebra, various antelope, and 200 bird species. Buffalo, black rhino and cheetah have been reintroduced.

www.sanparks.org

➕ 7C ✉ Eastern Cape ☎ 012-428 9111 ✋ Moderate

OUDTSHOORN AND CANGO CAVES

Oudtshoorn boomed between 1880 and 1914 when the ostrich feathers it produced were in huge demand. More recently it has rebuilt its fortunes through the export of ostrich meat and skins, and through tourism. In and around the town you can visit the lavish mansions of the ostrich barons, the excellent **C P Nel Museum,** showing the history of Oudtshoorn, and ostrich farms which display the whole life cycle of the birds.

About 30km (18.5 miles) from Oudtshoorn are the spectacular **Cango Caves,** with their huge caverns, limestone stalactites and dramatic dripstone formations. The cave system extends 2km (1.25 miles) into the hills.

www.oudtshoorn.com

➕ 5B ✉ Western Cape

ℹ Baron Van Rheede Street

☎ 044-279 2532 🕐 8–6

C P Nel Museum

✉ 3 Baron Van Rheede Street

☎ 044-272 7306;

www.cpnelmuseum.co.za

🕐 Mon–Fri 8–5; Sat 9–4

✋ Inexpensive

Cango Caves

☎ 044-272 7410;

www.cangocaves.co.za

🕐 9–4 ✋ Moderate 🍴 Restaurant (££)

PORT ELIZABETH

The Governor of the Cape, Sir Rufane Donkin, named this port in honour of his wife commemorating her with a small stone pyramid in the Donkin Reserve, in front of the Lighthouse. The chief attractions of the city, which forms part of the metropolitan area of Nelson Mandela Bay, are Bayworld Aquarium's seal and dolphin shows, the Snake Park, the Campanile Clock Tower, 56m (184ft) high and housing a carillon of 23 bells, and the Port Elizabeth Museum. About 50km (31 miles) south of the town are two of the world's finest surfing beaches, at St Francis Bay and Jeffreys Bay.

www.nelsonmandelatourism.co.za

✚ 7B ✉ Eastern Cape

ℹ Historical lighthouse buildings, Donkin Reserve ☎ 041-585 8884

Oceanarium (part of Bayworld)

✉ Beach Road, Humewood ☎ 041-584 0650; www.bayworld.co.za

🕘 9–4:30 👋 Moderate 🍴 Café (£)

RHODES MEMORIAL

Perched on the slopes of Devil's Peak, this classical-style memorial to the mining magnate, politician and imperialist Cecil Rhodes (1853–1902) is a favourite resort for Capetonians. The views are magnificent, children clamber over the bronze lions and visitors can lunch at the restaurant. The imposing granite monument was designed by Rhodes's favourite architect, Sir Herbert Baker. G F Watts sculpted the dramatic equestrian statue here called *Energy*, and Rudyard Kipling composed the poem inscribed below the bust of Rhodes.

✚ 27T ⊠ Off Rhodes Drive, on Groote Schuur Estate, Western Cape
🕐 Daylight hours 🖐 Free 🍴 Rhodes Memorial Restaurant 🕐 9–5
☎ 021-689 9151

ROBBEN ISLAND

Best places to see, ➤ 50–51.

STELLENBOSCH

Founded in 1679, this oak tree-filled town is home to Stellenbosch University and many other educational institutions, and is the centre of the Western Cape wine industry. Visitors come to see the wine estate in the surrounding countryside and the town's many museums and beautiful thatched and whitewashed Cape Dutch buildings. Take a walk along Dorp Street to see some of the best examples, stopping off at **Oom Samie Se Winkel,** a fascinating shop that's an attraction in its own right. The drive from Stellenbosch over the mountains to the Franschhoek valley takes you over the Helshoogte Pass, through oak groves and vineyards.
www.stellenboschtourism.co.za

✚ 2A ⊠ Western Cape
ℹ 36 Market Street ☎ 021-883 3584 🕐 Mon–Sat 9–5; Sun 10–4
Oom Samie Se Winkel
⊠ 84 Dorp Street ☎ 021-887 2372 🕐 Mon–Fri 8:30–5:30, Sat–Sun 9–5

SWELLENDAM

Situated below the Langeberg Mountains among shady oaks, the town of Swellendam, founded in 1745, has many fine Cape Dutch and Victorian houses. Swellendam's most striking building is the unusually ornate Dutch Reformed church. The old *drostdy* (house and office of the *landdrost*, or magistrate), dating from 1747, houses the Drostdy Museum, with its fine display of 18th- and 19th-century furniture.

www.swellendamtourism.co.za

✚ 4A ✉ Western Cape

ℹ Oefeninghuis, Voortrek Street ☎ 028-514 2770 🕐 Mon–Fri 8–5; Sat 9–12

TULBAGH

Tulbagh was almost destroyed by an earthquake in 1969, but has been painstakingly restored to its 18th-century appearance. The town's buildings constitute its main attraction, in particular the **De Oude Drostdy** (The Old Magistrate's Court), built in 1804 and now a museum. Also worth a visit is the Oude Kerk Volksmuseum, with displays on the life and material culture of a small Cape country town, and on the 1969 earthquake.

www.tulbaghtourism.org.za

✚ 3B ✉ Western Cape

ℹ 4 Kerk Street ☎ 023-230 1348 🕐 Mon–Fri 9–5; Sat 10–4, Sun 11–4

De Oude Drostdy

✉ Main Road (about 4km/2.5 miles) on Winterhoek Road) ☎ 023-230 1086 🕐 Mon–Sat 10–1, 2–5; Sun 2:30–5 ✋ Inexpensive ❓ Free wine-tasting

WILD COAST

This stretch of the Eastern Cape coast is one of the most scenic yet least visited parts of South Africa. There are reasons for this: the roads from the N2 down to the tiny coastal resorts are often extremely bad. But it is well worth the effort to visit places such as Qora Mouth, Mazeppa Bay, Coffee Bay and the larger town of Port St Johns. You will find deserted beaches, wide river mouths, mountainous sand dunes, stretches of virgin coastal forest – and delicious seafood.

➕ 10–11C ✉ Eastern Cape
ℹ 043-701 9600; www.ectourism.co.za

HOTELS

CAPE TOWN AND THE SURROUNDS

Cape Town Hollow Boutique Hotel (££)

This four-star hotel is very centrally located, right next to the Company's Garden (➤ 79). À la carte restaurants.

✉ 88 Queen Victoria Street, Cape Town, Western Cape ☎ 021-423 1260; www.capetownhollow.co.za

Lord Nelson Inn (£)

This welcoming three-star inn has a prime location on the Simon's Town waterfront, close to the Boulder penguin colony.

✉ 58 St George's Street, Simon's Town, Western Cape ☎ 021-786 1386

Mount Nelson (£££)

Arguably the country's most prestigious hotel, 'the Nellie' is a beautiful colonial-style building set in lush gardens.

✉ 76 Orange Street, Cape Town, Western Cape ☎ 021-483 1000; www.mountnelson.co.za

Twelve Apostles Hotel & Spa (£££)

This five-star boutique hotel has a stunning location on the west side of the peninsula. Exceptionally stylish rooms and food.

✉ Hout Bay Road, 2km south of Camp's Bay, Western Cape ☎ 021-437 9000; www.12apostleshotel.com

Vineyard Hotel & Spa (££–£££)

An excellent hotel with spectacular mountain views, a strong sense of history (the original building dates to 1799), and exquisite gardens leading. Gourmet restaurant, Au Jardin.

✉ Colinton Road, Newlands, Cape Town, Western Cape ☎ 021-683 3044; www.vineyard.co.za

EAST LONDON

Esplanade (££)

Affordable hotel in a good location right on the main beachfront. Special rates for children under the age of 16.

✉ 6 Clifford Street, Quigney, Beachfront, Eastern Cape ☎ 043-722 2518

FRANSCHHOEK
Franschhoek Country House (£££)
This restored manor house, set in tranquil gardens in the heart of the Cape Winelands, was once a perfumery. Pool and restaurant.
✉ Main Road, Franschhoek, Western Cape ☎ 021-876 3386; www.fch.co.za

GRAAFF-REINET
Drostdy Hotel (££–£££)
An elegant, old-world hotel with impeccable service and a comfortable atmosphere. Centrally located.
✉ 30 Church Street, Graaff-Reinet, Eastern Cape ☎ 049-892 2161; www.drostdy.com

GRAHAMSTOWN
Protea Hotel Grahamstown (££–£££)
Offers all the facilities you would expect from a hotel chain with an in-house family and an à la carte restaurant, as well as a bar.
✉ 123 High Street, Grahamstown, Eastern Cape ☎ 046-622 2324; www.proteahotels.com

KNYSNA
Knysna Log-Inn (££–£££)
Just a few hundred metres from the waterfront and the town centre. Unusual wooden hotel with a striking glassed front.
✉ 16 Gray Street, Knysna, Western Cape (Garden Route) ☎ 044-382 5835; www.kli.co.za

MATJIESFONTEIN
Lord Milner Hotel (££)
The whole village of Matjiesfontein has been declared a national monument, including this gracious Victorian hotel.
✉ Logan Road, Matjiesfontein, Western Cape ☎ 023-561 3011; www.matjiesfontein.com

PAARL
Oak Tree Lodge (££)
The lodge has spectacular views of the vineyards and Paarl

Mountain, with intimate private bathrooms. Near the Paarl
winelands and numerous hiking trails. Swimming pool.

✉ 32 Main Street, Paarl, Western Cape ☎ 021-863 2631;
www.oaktreelodge.co.za

PLETTENBERG BAY
Fynbos Ridge Cottages (££)

These exclusive Cape Dutch-style cottages are set amid beautiful
surroundings just ten minutes' drive from the beachfront.

✉ Plettenberg Bay, Western Cape ☎ 044-532 7855; www.fynbosridge.co.za

PORT ELIZABETH
Beach Hotel (££)

On the beachfront, near Bayworld and close to the shopping
centre. Safe swimming, surfing and sailing. Veranda restaurant.

✉ Marine Drive, Port Elizabeth, Eastern Cape ☎ 041-583 2161

STELLENBOSCH
D'Ouwe Werf (££–£££)

South Africa's oldest inn, founded in 1802, is an original Cape
Dutch building. Good restaurant and a good base for wine routes.

✉ 30 Church Street, Western Cape ☎ 021-887 4608; www.ouwewerf.com

SWELLENDAM
Swellengrebel Hotel (££)

Comfortable luxury rooms available at this hotel en route from
Cape Town to the Garden Route.

✉ 91 Voortrek Street, Swellendam, Western Cape ☎ 028-514 1144;
www.swellengrbelhotel.co.za

RESTAURANTS

CAPE TOWN AND THE SURROUNDS
Africa Café (£–££)

Provides authentic African food, serving a buffet of meat dishes as
well as Kenyan vegetable pâtés or Moroccan couscous salad.

✉ 108 Shortmarket Street, Cape Town, Western Cape ☎ 021-422 0221
🕐 Daily dinner

Aubergine (££–£££)

Classic cuisine served al fresco in a shady courtyard. South African specialties, as well as dishes such as quail and aubergine soufflé.

✉ 39 Barnet Street Gardens, Cape Town, Western Cape ☎ 021-465 4909
🕐 Mon–Sat dinner; Thu lunch only

Bertha's (££)

Likeable, attractively positioned seafront bar and eatery in Simon's Town. The speciality is seafood (try the mixed platter).

✉ Wharf Rd, Simon's Town, Western Cape ☎ 021-786 2138 🕐 Times vary

Cape Colony Restaurant (£££)

Beautifully proportioned interior with a mural of old Cape Town and a domed ceiling. The food is exceptionally good.

✉ Mount Nelson Hotel, 76 Orange Street, Cape Town, Western Cape
☎ 021-483 1000 🕐 Daily dinner

Constantia Uitsig (££–£££)

Set in beautiful vineyards, this restaurant is consistently rated one of Cape Town's best. The menu features excellent red meat, seafood and pasta dishes.

✉ Uitsig Farm, Constantia, Western Cape ☎ 021-794 1810 🕐 Sat and Sun lunch and dinner. Closed Jul

Morituri (£)

If you're on a low budget and you're looking for pizza, this restaurant serves the best in town.

✉ 214 Main Road, Claremont, Western Cape ☎ 021-683 6671 🕐 Mon–Fri lunch, dinner

Savoy Cabbage (££–£££)

Fresh food simply cooked is the motto of this outstanding restaurant. Serves fine seafood dishes and great desserts.

✉ 101 Hout Street, Cape Town, Western Cape ☎ 021-424 2626 🕐 Mon–Fri lunch; Mon–Sat dinner

FRANSCHHOEK
Monneaux (£££)
Monneaux is one of the country's top restaurants; the emphasis here is on international cuisine and local wines.

✉ Franschhoek Country House, Main Road, Western Cape ☎ 021-876-3386
🕐 Daily lunch; Mon–Sat dinner

KNYSNA
The Pink Umbrella (£–££)
Al fresco dining in summer in the beautiful garden, or in the pleasant dining room. Vegetarian meals a specialty.

✉ 14 Kingsway, Leisure Island, Knysna, Western Cape (Garden Route)
☎ 044-384 0135 🕐 Daily lunch, dinner.

MONTAGU
Four Oaks Restaurant (££)
An elegant restaurant housed in a mid-19th-century thatched cottage. Regularly changing menu, good on South African dishes.

✉ 46 Long Street, Montagu, Western Cape ☎ 023-614 2778 🕐 Daily dinner

PAARL
Rhebokskloof Estate (££–£££)
Restaurant on a beautiful out-of-town wine estate, with a menu ranging from soups and fresh salads to grilled fish and meat.

✉ Rhebokskloof Estate, North Paarl, Western Cape ☎ 021-869 8606
🕐 Tue–Thu lunch; Thu–Mon dinner

STELLENBOSCH
De Kelder Restaurant (££–£££)
The oldest eatery in Stellenbosch is set in the heart of the town.

✉ 69 Dorp Street, Western Cape ☎ 021-883 3797 ☎ Daily lunch, dinner

SWELLENDAM
Zanddrift (££)
Set in an 18th-century cottage, this restaurant in the Drostdy Museum (► 102) offers excellent country-fresh fare.

✉ Swellengrebel Street, Western Cape ☎ 028-514 1789 🕐 Daily

TULBAGH
Paddagang Wine House (£)
Cape farmhouse fare served either in an old thatched wine house
or under a shady pergola; very good wine list.
✉ 21 Church Street, Tulburgh, Western Cape ☎ 023-230 0242 ◷ Daily
breakfast, lunch, teas

PLETTENBERG BAY
Moby Dick's Restaurant & Deck (££)
Seafood is the specialty at this open-decked restaurant on
Robberg Beach, but also serves local Karoo lamb and ostrich.
✉ Central Beach, Plettenberg Bey, Western Cape (Garden Route)
☎ 044-533 3682 ◷ Daily

EAST LONDON
Smokey Swallows (££)
Pan-seared tuna with wasabi mayonnaise is a specialty at this
restaurant, offering international cuisine and live jazz on Sundays.
✉ 20 Devereaux Avenue, Eastern Cape ☎ 043-727 1349 ◷ Daily 11–11

PORT ELIZABETH
Mauro's (££–£££)
The menu at this brightly decorated restaurant offers a good range
of Mediterranean dishes. Great view over Kings Beach.
✉ McArthur Bath Complex, Beach Road ☎ 041-582 2700/582 4910
◷ Mon–Fri lunch, Mon–Sat dinner

SHOPPING

Cavendish Square
This is a classy shopping centre in the southern suburbs.
✉ Dreyer Street, Claremont, Cape Town, Western Cape ☎ 021-657 5600

Greenmarket Square
See page 81.

Green Point Flea Market
Huge Sunday flea market with everything from bric-à-brac to

antiques and curios. Good bargain hunting.

⊠ Next to Green Point Stadium, Cape Town, Western Cape ☀ Sun

St George's Mall

Pedestrian mall in the centre of Cape Town, with numerous arts
and craft stalls, as well as curios and original artworks for sale.

⊠ St George's Mall, Cape Town, Western Cape

Long Street

See page 82.

Victoria & Alfred Waterfront

See Best places to see, ➤ 54–55.

Tygervalley Centre

Large mall just outside Cape Town. Department stores, cinemas,
restaurants, a supermarket and a variety of specialty shops.

⊠ Tygervalley Centre, Bezuidenhout Avenue, Bellville, Cape Town, Western
Cape ☎ 021-914 1822

ENTERTAINMENT

Artscape Theatre Complex

Large complex with several performance areas, featuring dance,
plays, musicals, concerts and opera.

⊠ D F Malan Street, Cape Town ☎ 021-421 7695; www.artscape.co.za

Manenburg Jazz Café

Recently relocated to the Waterfront, this is a legendary location
for local jazz, especially at weekends.

⊠ Clock Tower Centre, V&A Waterfront, Cape Town, Western Cape
☎ 021-421 5639 ☀ Daily

Rhodes House

Expensive, but internationally highly rated nightclub housed in an
historic monument. Offers R&B, hip-hop, and themed evenings.

⊠ 60 Queen Victoria Street, Cape Town, Western Cape ☎ 021-424 8844
☀ Dec–Apr Mon–Sat; May–Nov Thu and Sat

Northeast Region

**This region includes a
variety of landscapes:
hundreds of kilometres of
subtropical coastline, the
rolling hills of the KwaZulu-
Natal Midlands, the
uKhahlamba-Drakensberg
and Soutpansberg
mountains, and the
open savannah of
eastern Mpumalanga. The
diversity of the landscape is
matched by the diversity of its
peoples: Zulu, Ndebele, Venda, Tsonga, English- and
Afrikaans-speaking whites, and a sizeable Indian
population, mainly in KwaZulu-Natal. The chief urban
centres are Durban, Pietermaritzburg, Nelspruit and
Polokwane (formerly Pietersburg).**

Durban

The glory of the region is its outstanding game reserves. Visitors
flock to the Kruger National Park in the hope of seeing Africa's Big

Five, and to the Blyde River
Canyon for its breathtaking
views. Black and white rhino
are the main attraction of
Hluhluwe-Imfolozi Game
Reserve, while hippo,
pelican and flamingo draw
naturelovers to the Greater
St Lucia Wetland Park,
designated a World Heritage
Site in 1999.

DURBAN

Durban's fine beaches and many hotels make it South Africa's premier tourist resort. Named in 1835 after the Governor of the Cape Sir Benjamin D'Urban, this fast-growing city is known to local Zulu people as eThekwini (Place of Sea). Like most urban centres in South Africa, it is a mixture of downtown skyscrapers and neat middle-class suburbs, with sprawling townships and shanty towns around the perimeter. With its superb natural harbour, it has long been the country's largest, busiest port.

Although Durban can be uncomfortably hot and humid in midsummer, for most of the year it enjoys wonderfully mild, sunny weather. The city is very much geared to low- and middle-income tourism, with many activities along the beachfront. Water sports, fishing, golf, shops, restaurants, rickshaw rides, snake parks – Durban has them all.

✚ 12E ✉ KwaZulu-Natal

African Arts Centre

Officially listed as a non-profit organization, this centre is an excellent place to buy traditional African art from the townships around the city, the long-established arts centre at Rorke's Drift and all parts of KwaZulu-Natal. Here you can find many kinds of beadwork, baskets, pottery, woodcarvings, textiles and wire sculptures. The centre also provides information about other African art outlets in the area.

www.durbanexperience.co.za;
www.afriart.org.za

✉ 94 Florida Rd, Morningside
☎ 031-312 3804 ⏰ Mon–Sat 9–6
🖐 Free

Botantic Gardens

An ivory hunter named John
Cane originally owned the land
on which these gardens were
laid out in 1848. They contain
beautiful stands of striped green
and yellow bamboo, old cycads,
fine established trees and a
scent garden for the blind.
One of the highlights is the
collection of orchids.

✉ 70 St Thomas Road ☎ 031-309
1271 ⏰ 7:30–5:15 🖐 Free
🍴 Snack bar (£)

City Hall and Museums

Belfast in Northern Ireland provided the model for Durban's elaborate City Hall, built in 1910. The result is an interesting example of colonial baroque, set amid graceful palm trees. Within the same building and city block are several museums and galleries.

The **Durban Art Gallery** has a good collection of Victorian painting, contemporary South African art, Chinese ceramics and Lalique glass from France. In the **Natural Science Museum** you can see realistic displays of stuffed birds, reptiles, fishes and insects, as well as a dodo skeleton and an ancient Egytian mummy. The nearby **Old Court House Museum** houses fascinating displays relating to the social, economic and political history of Durban.

Art Gallery & Museums

✉ West Street ☎ 031-311 2264 (Art Gallery); 031-311 2256 (Natural Science Museum); 031-311 2229 (Old Court House Museum) ⏰ Mon–Sat 8:30–4, Sun 11–4 ✋ Free 🍴 Café in Natural Science Museum (£)

Golden Mile

This stretch of beachfront running northward from Addington Beach to Blue Lagoon is the heart of Durban's tourist area. Many hotels and blocks of holiday apartments line the strip. Sightseers stroll up and down the promenade, swimmers enjoy a dip in the warm Indian Ocean and surfers ride the well-formed waves, while sun-worshippers soak up the rays. On the Golden Mile you can

take a rickshaw ride, visit the amusement park or buy African art from pavement vendors. However, be on your guard; many petty thieves and pickpockets operate here.

✉ Marine Parade
🏠 160 Pine Street ☎ 031-304 4934
⏰ Mon–Fri 8–4.30; Sat 9–2

Killie Campbell Collections

Muckleneuk, the mansion built by the sugar baron Sir Marshall Campbell, is home to the superb Killie Campbell Africana Collection. Campbell's daughter, Margaret Roach (Killie) Campbell, collected prints, artefacts, pictures, books and maps relating to Africa, particularly KwaZulu-Natal and its tribes, and these now form the core of the collection. Noteworthy are the several hundred paintings of tribal dress by local artist Barbara Tyrrell, and the displays of Zulu beadwork. The gardens around the house are particularly beautiful, landscaped in Victorian style.

✉ 220 Marriott Road ☎ 031-260 1722 ⏰ By appointment ✋ Moderate

Kwamuhle Museum

The name KwaMuhle ('place of the good one') commemorates J S Marwick, an official who helped thousands of Zulus return to their homes from the Transvaal during the Anglo-Boer War. The museum occupies the former offices of the Bantu Administration Board. Its displays show the social history of South African cities, Durban in particular, from the perspective of the black majority.

✉ 130 Ordinance Road ☎ 031-311 2223 🕐 Mon–Sat 8:30–4 ✋ Free

Shree Ambalavaanar Alayam Hindu Temple

This temple on Bellair Road, 3km (2 miles) west of the city centre, is the site of a fire-walking ceremony held each Easter and attended by thousands, both Hindu and non-Hindu. All are

welcome to attempt the barefoot crossing of the pits filled with glowing embers. The temple is just one sign of the substantial Indian presence in Durban. From 1860 to 1911 some 152,000 Indians came to KwaZulu-Natal, most to work as

indentured labourers in the sugar-cane plantations, often under appalling conditions. Among the immigrants was Gandhi.

The area around Grey Street, in the city centre, is the heart of the Indian business district. The shops here, selling a range of spices and curry powders, imported Indian brasswork and bright, cheerful textiles, are well worth a visit.

Hindu Temple

✉ 890 Bellair Road ☎ 031-261 5030 🕐 Daily 10–5 🖐 Free

Ushaka Marine World

Three distinct areas make up this new complex. uShaka Sea World comprises one of the finest aquariums in the country. On display here are turtles, many types of tropical fish, and most of the species of sharks found in KwaZulu-Natal waters. Swimmers needn't worry though – all the main beaches are fully protected by shark nets. uShaka Village Walk is a collection of restaurants and shops, while uShaka Wet 'n Wild World has water rides and slides.

www.ushakamarineworld.co.za

✉ 1 Bell Street, Point ☎ 031–328 8000 🕐 Daily 9–5 🖐 Expensive

through the Valley of a Thousand Hills

This drive takes you through the scenic hill country west of Durban, dotted with traditional Zulu homesteads.

Take the N3 out of Durban in the direction of Pietermaritzburg, then the M13 towards Pinetown and Kloof. Just after Kloof take the turn-off on to the R103 in the direction of Hillcrest. You are now on a stretch of the Old Main Road from Durban to Pietermaritzburg. Continue on to Botha's Hill.

At Botha's Hill there are excellent views over the Valley of a Thousand Hills. You can also visit Phezulu Safari Park, a re-creation of a Zulu village, with traditional Zulu dancing and a craft centre.

Continue on the R103 for 5km (3 miles) and turn right to the Rob Roy Hotel.

Have lunch or tea at the hotel, a strange European fantasy in the middle of rural KwaZulu-Natal. Outstanding scenic viewpoints can be found at the hotel and about 700m (763 yards) past it on the same road.

Return to the R103 and drive to Drummond.

There are wonderful vistas of the Valley of a Thousand Hills from the town and from around it. As you drive the R103 spare a thought for the athletes who run this way each year in the Comrades Marathon between Durban and Pietermaritzburg.

The R103 winds on through Inchanga and Cato Ridge. At Camperdown turn on to the N3 and return to Durban on the highway.

This route takes you through attractive low hills and grassland back into the city.

Distance 120km (74 miles)
Time 1.5 hours without stops, 4 hours with stops
Start/end point Durban city centre ✚ 12E
Lunch or tea Rob Roy Hotel (£–££) ☎ 031-777-1305

Phezulu Safari Park
✉ 5 Old Main Road, Botha's Hill ☎ 031-777 1000;
www.phezulusafaripark.co.za ⏰ Daily 8:30–5

More to see in the Northeast Region

BARBERTON

Cockney Liz and Florrie the Golden Dane were just two of the 'good-time girls' attracted to this place when gold was discovered here in 1884. Barberton, named after the Barber cousins who discovered the main ore-bearing reef, expanded into a warren of bars, gambling halls, canteens and stock exchanges in just two years, but the town's economy collapsed when the miners moved to the richer diggings of the Witwatersrand. A number of buildings from the boom days have been preserved, including the Transvaal's first Stock Exchange, the 1887 Globe Tavern, Belhaven House and Stopforth House (1886). **Barberton Museum** highlights the gold rush and the geology of the area. In front of the town hall a statue of Jock of the Bushveld, a Staffordshire bull terrier, commemorates the eponymous hero of Percy Fitzpatrick's novel.
www.barberton.info

➕ 23J ✉ Mpumalanga
ℹ Market Place ☎ 013-712 2121 ⏰ Mon–Fri 8:30–5; Sat, Sun 9–3

Barberton Museum

 ✉ 36 Pilgrim Street ☎ 013-712 4208 🕐 Daily 9–4 ✋ Free ❓ Phone for details of tours of historic houses

BLYDE RIVER CANYON
Best places to see, ➤ 36–37.

DUNDEE AND LADYSMITH BATTLEGROUNDS
Some of the most famous battles in South African history between Afrikaner and Zulu, Zulu and Briton, and Briton and Afrikaner were fought on KwaZulu-Natal territory. In the region around Dundee you can visit Isandlwana Historic Reserve, where Zulu warriors inflicted a heavy defeat on the British army during the Anglo-Zulu War of 1879, and Rorke's Drift, where the British repulsed a strong Zulu attack. Also in this area is Blood River. Here 64 bronze ox-wagons mark the place where a Boer commando of 464 men and 64 wagons, led by Andries Pretorius, defeated a Zulu force of 3,000 in 1838.

In and around Ladysmith are many memorials to the Anglo-Boer War. **Ladysmith Siege Museum** has displays relating to the siege of the British in the town by the Boers, which lasted for nearly four

months from 1899 into 1900. Anglo-Boer War sites nearby include Wagon Hill, 5km (3 miles) south of Ladysmith, and Spioenkop, off the R60, west of town.

www.ladysmith.co.za; www.tourdundee.co.za

✚ 22G–H ✉ KwaZulu-Natal

ℹ Dundee Tourist Information: Victoria Street

🕐 Mon–Fri 9–4:45; Sat 9–12 ☎ 034-212 2121;

ℹ Ladysmith Tourist Information ☎ 036-637 2992

Ladysmith Siege Museum

✉ Murchison Street, Ladysmith ☎ 036-637 2992

🕐 Mon–Fri 9–4; Sat 9–1

GREATER ST LUCIA WETLAND PARK

Best places to see, ➤ 44–45.

HLUHLUWE-IMFOLOZI NATIONAL PARK

Hluhluwe and Imfolozi, originally separate parks, have
been joined together by a corridor 8km (5 miles) wide to
create a single reserve. The park encompasses many
habitats – thick scrub, grassland, forest, savannah and woodland –
which in turn support a wide range of animals. Most famous are
the numerous white rhinos, bred here from the point of near
extinction. They share the park with black rhinos, the rest of the
Big Five (➤ 11), antelope, zebra, warthog, hippo and hundreds of
species of bird. You can book walking trails through the park.

✚ 23G ✉ KwaZulu-Natal ☎ 033-845 1003; book at www.kznwildlife.com
🕐 Mon–Fri 7–5, Sat 7–3 ✋ Moderate

KRUGER NATIONAL PARK

Best places to see, ➤ 46–47.

LETABA

This district, around the town of Tzaneen, has several attractive spots to visit. The Modjadji Nature Reserve, cut through by several walking trails, supports the world's largest concentration of cycads, strange primitive plants unchanged in form for millions of years. The cycads here are sacred to the Modjadji Rain Queen, an existing matriarchy (the incumbent queen took the throne in 2003) said to have been the inspiration for Rider Haggard's novel *She*. A short drive from Tzaneen will take you through tea estates, eucalyptus plantations and indigenous forest to Magoebaskloof Dam and the Debengeni Falls. Another popular resort in the area is the Fanie Botha Dam.

www.tzaneeninfo.co.za

✚ 22L ✉ Limpopo Province

🛈 25 Danie Joubert Street ☎ 015-307 6513 🕐 Mon–Fri 8–5; Sat 8–11

MAPUNGUBWE NATIONAL PARK

One of South Africa's most under-publicized historical sites is the magnificent ruined stone city of Mapungubwe, set on a remote hilltop overlooking the Limpopo River on the border with Zimbabwe. The city was founded circa AD1220 as the capital of a complex Bantu society whose income derived from gold mining and the transportation of this product to the maritime trade emporium of Kilwa on the East Africa's Swahili Coast. Mapungubwe was abandoned circa 1290, when an even grander capital was built about 300km (180 miles) northeast at Great Zimbabwe. Among the wealth of artefacts discovered here are a pair of golden rhinos now housed in a museum at the University of Pretoria.

Unseen by Europeans until the 1930s, Mapungubwe was initially accorded official protection in 1947, but was delisted a year later by the freshly installed Nationalist Party, since its very existence was at odds with the racist assumptions that informed apartheid orthodoxy. Mapungubwe was finally reincorporated into the national parks system in 1995, recognized as a World Heritage Site in 2002, and finally opened to the public in 2004 following the construction of a rest camp with simple tented accommodation and a campsite. Although some wildlife occurs in the area, it is the only South African national park to be formed primarily for its historical and cultural significance, which also includes several rock art shelters. Though small, the park is of great interest to birders with more than 400 species recorded, several hides, and a superb tree-top boardwalk.

www.sanparks.org

✚ 22M ✉ Limpopo Province ☎ 012-428 9111 🕓 Daily, daylight hours 🖐 Expensive

PIETERMARITZBURG AND THE MIDLANDS

Named after the Voortrekker leaders Piet Retief and Gerrit Maritz, Pietermaritzburg was made capital of Britain's Natal Colony in 1838, and it remains provincial capital of KwaZulu-Natal today. Often abbreviated to 'Maritzburg, the city is also known as uMgungundlovu, the official Zulu name of the local district municipality, meaning 'Place of the Elephant'. Pietermaritzburg's architecture retains a colonial feel: a stroll around Church Street will take you past the magnificent redbrick City Hall, the historic Supreme Court and the Legislative Assembly Building of 1889. A strong Indian and Islamic presence is represented by the Ghandi Statue near the City Hall, the Top Mosque off Church Street and the Hindu Temple on the corner of Williams and Longmarket. Pietermaritzburg offers easy access to the KwaZulu-Natal Midlands, an area of pretty green rolling hills that rises westward to the base of the mighty uKhahlamba-Drakensberg. Picnic at Midmar Dam, view the 95m (311ft) Howick Falls in the town of the same name, or follow the 'Midlands Meander' from Hilton to Hidcote, visiting arts and crafts studios and antiques shops.

www.pmbtourism.co.za

✚ 11E ✉ KwaZulu-Natal

🚹 177 Commercial Road ☎ 033-345 1348 🕐 Mon–Fri 8–5; Sat 8–3; Sun 9–3. Midlands Meander Information ☎ 033-330 8195; www.midlandsmeander.co.za

PILGRIM'S REST

The wood and corrugated-iron buildings of 19th-century Pilgrim's Rest show what life was like in a mining camp of the old Transvaal. In 1873, Alec Patterson discovered South Africa's richest deposit of alluvial gold here. Although the focus of mining interest shifted to the Witwatersrand, extraction of gold continued here into the 20th century. Pilgrim's Rest has remained virtually intact and can be seen on a walking tour (➤ 126–127).

www.pilgrimsrest.org.za

✚ 23K ✉ Mpumalanga

🚹 082-456 8345

a walk around Pilgrim's Rest

This walk takes you through the historic centre of the old mining town of Pilgrim's Rest (► 125).

Start where the road from Sabie enters the town's main street. You will see a succession of historic buildings on your left.

First is the small Anglican Church of St Mary, made of brick. Next comes the corrugated-iron Town Hall, followed by Leadley's Building. If you look towards the creek on your right, you will see some of the old alluvial diggings. From here on in quick succession are: the Old Print House, now a shop; the Pilgrim's and Sabie News; and the European Hotel.

At this point bear right along the curving stretch of road leading to the Tourist Information Centre.

On your right is a house with a wide veranda. This is Chaitow, named after its former owner, the jack-of-all-trades C H Chaitow. Next on the right is the Information Centre, where you can buy a ticket for admission to all the town's museums. The Royal Hotel, opposite, has displays of old mining gear.

Walk on past the Information Centre, continuing to bear right.

The old post office on the left is now a museum. Opposite, to the right, is the Miner's House Museum, which demonstrates the lifestyle of a miner in the 1910s.

If you have the time, get a map from the Information Centre and take the longer walk to see the historic Cemetery, the Central Reduction Works and the stone-built Joubert Bridge.

Distance 2km (1.25 miles)
Time 1 hour without stops, 3 hours with stops
Start point Where the Sabie road enters Pilgrim's Rest ✚ 23K
End point Miner's House Museum
Lunch or tea The Vine (££) ☎ 013-768 1080

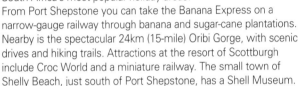

PORT SHEPSTONE AND THE HIBISCUS COAST

The chain of seaside resorts strung out along the coast south of Durban is one of South Africa's most popular holiday areas.

From Port Shepstone you can take the Banana Express on a narrow-gauge railway through banana and sugar-cane plantations. Nearby is the spectacular 24km (15-mile) Oribi Gorge, with scenic drives and hiking trails. Attractions at the resort of Scottburgh include Croc World and a miniature railway. The small town of Shelly Beach, just south of Port Shepstone, has a Shell Museum.

www.hibiscuscoast.kzn.org.za

✚ 11–12D ⊠ KwaZulu-Natal

🛈 Port Shepstone Tourist Information: Princess Elizabeth Drive

☎ 039-682 2455

🛈 South Coast Tourist Information: Panorama Parade, Margate Beachfront

☎ 039-312 2322 ⏰ Mon–Fri 8–4:30; Sat 9–11

SUDWALA CAVES

These caves, in Mankelekele Mountain, were formed by the action of water percolating through the dolomitic rock. They are named after Sudwala, a Swazi who took refuge here in the 19th century. Only 600m (654 yards) of the vast cave system are open to the public, but guided tours take you through passages into large chambers where fantastic dripstone formations can be seen. On the ceiling are the round shapes of fossilized stromalites, algae which were among the earliest living organisms on earth.

www.sudwalacaves.co.za

✚ 22K ⊠ About 35km (22 miles) northwest of Nelspruit, off the R539, Mpumalanga ☎ 013-733 4152 ⏰ Daily 8:30–4:30 🍴 Restaurant (££), café (£) 🎟 Moderate

TONGAAT AND THE DOLPHIN COAST

Though less built up than the South Coast, the coast north of Durban also has several very popular tourist resorts. Umhlanga Rocks offers large tourist hotels, seafood restaurants and the nearby **Natal Sharks Board,** which features an audio-visual presentation on sharks and an impressive array of fibreglass casts taken directly from captured sharks.

In the mainly Indian town of Tongaat you can visit the country's oldest Hindu place of worship, the Juggernath Puri Temple, learn about the sugar industry at Hulett's Maidstone Mill, or see crocodiles at Crocodile Creek. All along the coast are excellent beaches and there is a good chance of seeing schools of dolphins.

www.thedolphincoast.co.za

✚ 12E ✉ KwaZulu-Natal

ℹ Dolphin Coast Publicity Association ☎ 032-946 1997

Natal Sharks Board

✉ 1A Herrwood Drive, Umhlanga Rocks ☎ 031-566 0400; www.shark.co.za

🕐 Presentation: Tue, Wed Thu at 9 and 2; Sun at 2

UKHAHLAMBA-DRAKENSBERG PARK

Best places to see, ➤ 52–53.

VENDA

The region of the Venda people in the Soutpansberg (Salt Pan Mountains) is famous for its rituals and sacred places. The holiest spot of all is Lake Fundudzi, said to have been the home of a fertility god in the form of a huge python. From the main urban centre of the area, Makhado (formerly Louis Trichardt), you can drive to the Hangklip Forest Reserve or through Wyllie's Poort.

✚ 23M ✉ Limpopo Province
ℹ Soutpansberg Tourism ☎ 015-516 0040;
www.tourismsoutpansberg.co.za

ZULULAND

The town of Eshowe is a good base for exploring the kingdom of Zululand, which reached the height of its power under Shaka in the early 19th century. The **Vukani Museum** and the Zululand Historical Museum in Fort Nonquai, with their displays of arts, crafts and furniture, give a good insight into Zulu culture. Re-creations of Zulu settlements can be seen at **Shakaland,** 14km (19 miles) from Eshowe, originally the set for the TV series *Shaka Zulu*, and at other cultural villages nearby.

✚ 23H ✉ KwaZulu-Natal
ℹ Eshowe Tourist Information ✉ Osbourne Road ☎ 035-474 1141 🕓 Mon–Fri 7:30–4

Vukani Museum
✉ Osbourne Street, Eshowe ☎ 035-474 5274 🕓 Daily 7:30–4

Shakaland
✉ Off the R66 between Eshowe and Melmoth ☎ 035-460 0912; www.shakaland.com 🕓 Mon–Fri 6am–9pm

an excursion to Swaziland

The 365sq km (142sq miles) Kingdom of Swaziland is surrounded on three sides by South Africa, and on the fourth by Mozambique. Linguistically, the people belong to the Nguni group, which includes the Xhosa and the Zulu of South Africa. The country is ruled by an absolute monarch, at present King Mswati III. Farming, forestry, mining and the export of labour to South Africa provide most of the country's income.

The capital, Mbabane, lies in a pleasant hilly setting. Don't miss its Swazi market, with fresh produce, woven items and handicrafts on sale. To the southeast is the Ezulwini Valley ('place of heaven'), which has several hotels, hot springs, a casino, Parliament and the Swazi royal residence at Lobamba. Mlilwane Wildlife Sanctuary (5,000ha/12,350 acres), also in the valley, is noted for the bird life around its several dams; many other animals which had virtually become extinct in the area have been reintroduced here, including hippo, eland, giraffe and warthog.

Two other reserves can be visited in lower-lying savannah of eastern Swaziland: the Hlane Royal National Park and the rugged Mkhaya Game Reserve, both of which have larger animals, such as elephant and rhino.

Piggs Peak in the mountainous northwest part of Swaziland, once a mining centre, is now a commercial forestry area. The district offers wonderful scenic drives and good hikes.

Swaziland is famous for two colourful annual ceremonies – the women's Umhlanga (reed) dance, and the young men's Ncwala (first fruits) ceremony.

www.welcometoswaziland.com

✚ 23J

ℹ Swaziland Tourist Information: 09268-403 9693 or 09268-404 9675

an excursion to Lesotho

The mountain kingdom of Lesotho, entirely surrounded by South Africa, owes its existence to the statesman Moshoeshoe (pronounced Moshwehshweh). Through much of the 19th century he managed to protect the Basotho people he had gathered together on the impregnable flat-topped hill, Thaba Bosiu ('mountain of the night'), against many enemies – other tribes, Boers, Britons. In 1884 the country came under British rule, and in 1966 it attained independence as a constitutional monarchy.

Almost all of Lesotho is rugged and mountainous, with few good roads. The country's great attraction is its spectacular

scenery, with many clear streams and rivers, sandstone caves (often covered with prehistoric rock art), and mountain slopes dotted with traditional homesteads. Multi-day, or shorter hiking, pony trekking and 4x4 trails are available, as are excellent opportunities for trout fishing and birdwatching. The country is known for its rugs and goods woven from grass, wool and mohair. Look for the distinctive Basotho grass hats – conical in shape with a large knob on top.

The Lesotho Highlands Water Scheme, a colossal engineering project of the late 20th century, has created the Katse Dam in the centre of Lesotho, which provides water to South Africa via an elaborate system of tunnels and canals. It can be reached by an excellent road, and the views are stunning.

Also worth visiting is the capital, Maseru, where you can buy arts and crafts. Thaba Bosiu, nearby, is a sacred place for the people of Lesotho; the graves of Moshoeshoe and other leading national figures are here.

www.mtec.gov.ls

✚ 10E

ℹ Ministry of Tourism: 7th Floor, Post Office Building, Kingsway, Maseru ☎ 09266-2231 1054

HOTELS

BARBERTON
Diggers Retreat (££)
Owner-run hotel with gold-panning and trips to Eureka City.
✉ Main Street, Barberton, Mpumalanga ☎ 013-719 9681

DURBAN
Albany Hotel (£–££)
Situated in the heart of Durban, this brightly restored art deco block offers air-conditioned rooms with TV, restaurant and pub.
✉ 225 Smith Street, Durban, KwaZulu-Natal ☎ 031-304 4381;
www.albanyhotel.co.za

Blue Waters Hotel (££)
Long-established hotel, on the beachfront, offering reasonably priced spacious, rooms with private balcony. Covered parking.
✉ 175 Snell Parade, Durban, KwaZulu-Natal ☎ 031-327 7000;
www.bluewatershotel.co.za

City Lodge Durban (£)
Close to the main Durban attractions. Spacious, comfortable rooms at very good rates. Secure parking and swimming pool.
✉ Corner of Brickhill and Old Fort roads, Durban, KwaZulu-Natal ☎ 031-332 1447; www.citylodge.co.za

Essenwood House (££)
Fine accommodation in a stylish Georgian manor overlooking the city and ocean; close to shopping mall. On-site pool and parking.
✉ 630 Essenwood Road, Durban, KwaZulu-Natal ☎ 031-207 4547 (and fax);
www.essenwoodhouse.co.za

HAZYVIEW
Farmhouse Country Lodge (££)
Near to the attractions of the area, this country house hotel offers a swimming pool, horse riding and hiking.
✉ 40km (25 miles) north of Nelspruit on Hazyview road, Mpumalanga
☎ 013-737 8780

Sabi River Sun (££–£££)

Safari hotel on the banks of the Sabi River, with thatched buildings set amid bushveld and a golf course. Barbecues are held in the *boma* (reeded enclosure) overlooking the river. Offers game drives.

✉ Main Sabie Road Hazyview, Mpumalanga ☎ 013-737 7311; www.southernsun.com

LIMPOPO PROVINCE
Tulani Safari Lodge (£££)

Luxurious thatched lodge in the heart of elephant country, within easy reach of the surrounding game.

✉ PO Box 148, Phalaborwa 1398, Limpopo Province ☎ C012-423 5610; www.tulanisafarilodge.co.za

Leokwe Camp (£-££)

This self-catering camp in Mapungubwe National Park has cottages, standing tents, camping sites, and a swimming pool.

✉ Limpopo Province ☎ 012-428 9111; www.sanparks.org

PIETERMARITZBURG AND THE MIDLANDS
Imperial Hotel (££)

Centrally located, Victorian hotel with elegant rooms and spacious surroundings. Bar and restaurant in-house.

✉ 224 Loop Street, Pietermaritzburg, KwaZulu-Natal ☎ 033-342 6551

Granny Mouse Country House (££)

Situated in the heart of the midlands, this legendary country retreat is renowned for its relaxed atmosphere, rambling opportunities, fine food and wellness centre/spa.

✉ Balgowan, 30 minutes' drive from Pietermaritzburg, KwaZulu-Natal ☎ 033-234 4071; www.grannymouse.co.za

PILGRIM'S REST
Royal Hotel (££)

Beautifully restored 19th-century buildings, now a national monument. Elegant rooms.

✉ PO Box 59, Pilgrims Rest 1290, Mpumalanga ☎ 013-768 1100

UKHAHLAMBA-DRAKENSBERG PARK

Cathedral Peak Hotel (££)

The only private hotel set within the park boundaries, this rambling family-oriented place offers accommodation of a high standard along with swimming, squash, horse riding, hiking.

✉ Cathedral Peak, Drakensberg, KwaZulu-Natal ☎ 036-488 1888; www.cathedralpeak.co.za

UMHLANGA ROCKS

Oyster Box (££)

Long-established, elegant, comfortable hotel with own swimming pool and well-known restaurant, the Oyster Box. Close to beach.

✉ 2 Lighthouse Road, Umhlanga Rocks, KwaZulu-Natal ☎ 031-561 2233; www.oysterbox.co.za

RESTAURANTS

DULLSTROOM

The Poacher (££)

This traditional Scottish-style hostelry serves country fare and pub food. The menu includes butternut soup, various trout dishes, rabbit and game pies, and Kassler rib (smoked pork chop).

✉ Dullstroom, DullStroom, Mpumalanga ☎ 013-254 0108 🕐 Mon–Sat lunch, dinner

DURBAN

Bean Bag Bohemia (££)

Good food in a mellow atmosphere. There's a separate bar area downstairs serving light meals, and a formal restaurant upstairs. Try the avocado *mille-feuille* or rabbit with ginger.

✉ 18 Windermere Road, Greyville, Durban, KwaZulu-Natal ☎ 031-309 6019 🕐 Daily lunch, dinner

The Edward Smorgasbord (££–£££)

This fabulous buffet, with a full range of seafood, is a Durban institution; set in the beautiful old, wood-panelled chartroom.

✉ Edward Hotel, 149 Marine Parade, Durban, KwaZulu-Natal ☎ 031-337 3681 🕐 Mon–Sat dinner

Little India (£)

With cooks from both North and South India, this restaurant offers a full range of Indian dishes, including excellent Tandoori chicken.

✉ 155 Musgrave Road, Musgrave, Durban, KwaZulu-Natal ☎ 031-201 1121
🕐 Daily lunch, dinner

Marco's (££–£££)

Modish Italian restaurant specializing in fresh home-made pastas and sauces. Try their duck ravioli or butternut panzerotti.

✉ 45 Windermere Road, Durban, KwaZulu-Natal ☎ 031-303 3078
🕐 Mon–Sat lunch; Sat dinner

Oyster Bar & Zenbi Sushi (££–£££)

Chic open-plan restaurant with great harbour view, good wine list, and fabulous seafood fresh from the Indian Ocean.

✉ Victoria Embankment, Durban, KwaZulu-Natal ☎ 031-307 7883 🕐 Daily lunch, dinner

HAZYVIEW/WHITE RIVER
Cybele Forest Lodge (£££)

This stylish restaurant serves a range of international dishes, with local specialties such as ostrich carpaccio. Reserve in advance.

✉ 26km (16 miles) outside White River, on R40 towards Hazyview, Mpumalanga ☎ 013-764 1823 🕐 Daily all day

LIMPOPO PROVINCE
Bergwater Restaurant (££)

Wonderful selection of seafood and traditional South African dishes.

✉ 5 Rissik Street, Makhado (formerly Louis Trichardt), Limpopo Province
☎ 015-516 0262 🕐 Daily all day

The Coach House (££–£££)

Housed in an old coaching inn, amid beautiful mountain scenery, the restaurant serves fine country fare.

✉ Agatha Road, near Tzaneen, Limpopo Province ☎ 015-306 8000
🕐 Daily all day

The Restaurant (££)

This restaurant in a Victorian house offers a variety of good food, ranging from Thai stir-fries to crêpes with spinach and feta filling.
✉ 50 Dorp Street, Polokwane (Peitersburg), Limpopo Province ☎ 015-291 1918 🕐 Mon–Fri lunch; Mon–Sat dinner

NELSPRUIT
Costa da Sol (££)

One of Nelspruit's top eateries, serving an extensive menu of grills and other dishes with a Portuguese influence.
✉ Absa Square, Paul Kruger Street, Mpumalanga ☎ 013-752 6382
🕐 Mon–Sat lunch, dinner

PIETERMARITZBERG AND THE MIDLANDS
Old Halliwell (££)

This charming country inn offers outdoor dining in summer and roaring fires in winter. Excellent international and local dishes.
✉ Curry's Post, Midlands, KwaZulu-Natal ☎ 033-330 0005 🕐 Tue–Sun breakfast, lunch and dinner

Rawdons Hotel (££–£££)

Stylish restaurant on a vast country estate specialising in country cooking, and traditional English pub serving locally brewed ales.
✉ Nottingham Road, Midlands, KwaZulu-Natal ☎ 033 263 6044; www.rawdons.co.za 🕐 Times vary

PILGRIM'S REST
Mount Sheba Hotel (£££)

Memorable five-course dinner menu, including local panfried trout, duck and smoked ostrich with cranberries. Excellent wines.
✉ Lydenburg Road, Pilgrim's Rest, Mpumalanga ☎ 013-768 1241 🕐 Daily. Reservations essential

SABIE
Blue Mountain Lodge (£££)

This lodge, set in an indigenous forest, offers the finest of regional fare on its changing seasonal menu.

✉ On the R514 to Kiepersol, Sabie, Mpumalanga ☎ 013-737 8446 ⏱ Daily. Reservations essential

The Woodsman (££)

Apart from panoramic views, this restaurant offers Greek-Cypriot cuisine as well as steaks, grilled fare and pub food.

✉ 94 Main Road, Sabie, Mpumalanga ☎ 013-764 2204 ⏱ Breakfast, lunch, dinner daily

UMHLANGA ROCKS

Razzmatazz (£–££)

The restaurant's wooden deck has a fine view of the beach, while the menu offers South African specialties. Try the crocodile kebab.

✉ Cabana Beach Resort, 10 Lagoon Drive, Umhlanga Rocks, KwaZulu-Natal ☎ 031-561 5847 ⏱ Daily lunch, dinner

SHOPPING

Amphitheatre Craft Market

This is one of Durban's oldest markets. Especially good for textiles and curios. Live jazz is played in the afternoon.

✉ Amphitheatre, North Beach, Durban, KwaZulu-Natal ☎ 031-328 3000 ⏱ Sun 9–5

Essenwood Craft Market

On offer are stained glass, decorative candles, clothing and a wide range of crafts.

✉ Corner of Essenwood and St Thomas roads, Durban, ZwaZulu-Natal ⏱ Sat 9–2

The Pavilion

This enormous, picturesque mall was built in the style of a Victorian conservatory.

✉ Spine Road, Westville, 10km west on the N3 from Durban city centre, Durban, KwaZulu-Natal ☎ 031-265 0558; www.thepav.co.za.

Victoria Street Market

Large, covered, mainly Indian market with many small outlets.

✉ Between Victoria and Queen Streets, Durban, KwaZulu-Natal

The Wheel

Popular mall with a nautical theme just behind the beachfront. A huge Ferris wheel gives the centre its name.

✉ 55 Gillespie Street, Durban, KwaZulu-Natal ☎ 031-332 4324

Gateway Mall

Although not central, this vast mall boasts the greatest concentration of shops and restaurants in Durban.

✉ M12, Umhlanga Rocks, Durban, KwaZulu-Natal ☎ 031-566 2332; www.gatewayworld.co.za

ENTERTAINMENT

Bat Centre

Art development and community centre with a restaurant, bar and a large auditorium, all offering regular performances of live music.

✉ 45 Maritime Place, Small Craft Harbour, Durban ☎ 031-332 0451

Rainbow Restaurant and Jazz Club

One of the oldest live jazz locales in the province. Phone for details of performances.

✉ Shop 6, 23 Stanfield Lane, Pinetown, Durban, Kwazulu-Natal
☎ 031-702 9161

Skido's

Popular alternative dance and rock music venue, live music a few nights every week.

✉ Corner of Clark /Umbilo Roads, Durban, Kwazulu-Natal
☎ www.undergroundpress.co.za

Tilt

Contemporary dance venue with well-known DJs playing the latest house, hip-hop and South African kwaito music.

✉ Walnut Street, Durban, Kwazulu-Natal ☎ www.clubtilt.co.za 🕓 Fri, Sat

Gauteng

Just 150 years ago, what is now the tiny province of Gauteng was home to scattered tribes, farmers, small Voortrekker towns and wild animals. Today, it is the economic powerhouse of South Africa, producing a third of the country's wealth, and home to its greatest concentration of city-dwellers. The reason for this dramatic change was the discovery of gold on the Witwatersrand (White Water Ridge) in 1886, which brought with it a massive influx of population and the rapid growth of cities.

Johannesburg

Gauteng – SeSotho for 'Place of Gold' – is now an almost continuous urban-industrial sprawl, from Vereeniging and Vanderbijlpark in the south, and Johannesburg and Soweto in the centre, to Pretoria in the north. For the visitor, the main attractions lie in the art galleries, museums, shops, theatres and restaurants of Johannesburg and Pretoria, and the people and historic interest of Soweto.

JOHANNESBURG

Although the seat of government lies elsewhere, Johannesburg is Southern Africa's largest city and the region's undisputed economic, industrial and financial capital.

Johannesburg (aka Joburg or Jozi) is a city built on gold – hence its African name, Egoli, 'place of gold'. An obscure prospector, George Harrison, first discovered the precious metal here in 1886. Within a year a mining town of 10,000 people had sprung up. By 1889 the young city had horse-drawn trams, and by 1890 electric lights. Soon fashionable suburbs appeared, such as Parktown (➤ 150) with its stone mansions. Nine years after the discovery of

gold the population of Johannesburg was 100,000; today it is several million. With the mines came many associated industries, commerce, financial institutions and a stock exchange which has grown into the largest in Africa.

Present-day Johannesburg is several cities in one. The original city centre, with its offices and skyscrapers, has the vibrant feel of an African city, its pavements abuzz with street vendors, many of whom originate from neighbouring countries. Because of the former policy of racial segregation, a separate black city, Soweto, has grown up to the southwest. Many big businesses and the stock exchange have recently moved north to the wealthy area of Sandton, where high-rise buildings are mushrooming.

Because of its wealth, Johannesburg has some of the country's finest and most expensive shops, some of its best museums, theatres and art galleries, and some of its most luxurious homes. But as in other South African cities, wealth exists alongside poverty and deprivation.

✚ 20J ✉ Gauteng

Apartheid Museum

This fine museum, opened by Nelson Mandela in 2002, has rapidly become a major tourist attraction. The museum offers a unique insight into South Africa's segregated past. Multimedia displays cover the rise of apartheid from 1948 on, black resistance to it, the release of Mandela in 1990, and the first democratic elections of 1994.

www.apartheidmuseum.org

✉ Next to Gold Reef City (► 146) ☎ 011-496 1822 🕐 Tue–Sun 10–5
✋ Moderate

Cradle of Humankind
Best places to see, ➤ 40–41.

Gold Reef City
Designed to give visitors the feel of 19th-century gold-mining Johannesburg, this theme park is built around an old mine, Crown Mines No.14 Shaft, which extends to depths of more than 3km (2 miles) below the surface. You can go more than 200m (656ft)

underground and experience what life was like for the early miners, and there are demonstrations of molten gold being poured to make ingots. Lining the reconstructed Victorian streets are shops, a hotel, a bank, a newspaper office, an antique apothecary's establishment, a laundry and a brewery. The park has fairground rides, and performances by African dance troupes.

www.goldreefcity.co.za

✉ Shaft 14, Northern Park Way, Ormonde ☎ 011-248 6800

🕙 Tue–Sun 9:30–5 💰 Expensive

🍴 Restaurants, pubs, café (£–££)

Johannesburg Art Gallery
Construction of this gallery, designed by Sir Edwin Lutyens and financed by Johannesburg's gold barons, began in 1915. The moving spirit behind its creation was the wife of one of the pioneers of the gold and diamond mining industry, Lady Philips. In line with the policy of most South African galleries, at first only European art was collected; the gallery owns a fine Rodin

sculpture and works by El Greco and Picasso. Later it acquired works by leading South African artists such as Pierneef, Irma Stern, Jackson Hlungwane and William Kentridge. Most recently the Brenthurst Collection of African art has been added.

✉ King George Street, Joubert Park ☎ 011-725 3130 🕔 Tue–Sun 10–5 ✋ Free

Johannesburg Zoo and Zoo Lake

Even if you don't like the idea of animals in enclosures, this zoo, which celebrated its centenary in 2004, is worth visiting for its lovely grounds. Indigenous animals such as lions, elephants and penguins can be seen, as well as exotic tapirs and polar bears.

Zoo Lake, across the road, is a favourite with locals wanting a day out, with spacious lawns for picnicking, a restaurant, and rowing boats for rent. Art exhibitions are held here monthly.

www.jhbzoo.org.za

✉ Jan Smuts Avenue, Parkview ☎ 011-646 2000 🕔 Daily 8:30–5:30 (no entry after 4) ✋ Moderate

Museumafrica

If you visit only one museum in South Africa, it should be this beautifully designed place. A number of smaller museums formerly dispersed through Johannesburg are housed together here under one roof. The Geological Museum has a wonderful display of rocks and crystals, while the Bensusan Museum of Photography fully illustrates the art of the camera from its beginnings to the present. The section called 'Johannesburg Transformations' is devoted to the history of the city and its inhabitants. Elsewhere you can see outstanding examples of prehistoric rock paintings and traditional African arts, with a wealth of information on the exhibits.

✉ 121 Bree Street ☎ 011-833 5624 ⏱ Tue–Sun 9–5 ✋ Inexpensive 🍴 Café (£)

Newtown Cultural Precinct

At the heart of this grouping of cultural facilities is the **Market Theatre,** which became famous under apartheid for its oppositional protest theatre. The theatre gets its name from the old fresh produce market in which it is built – make sure you take a

look at the fine 1911 beaux arts façade. The surrounding Precinct now includes several performance spaces, museums, music venues, an art gallery and a variety of places to eat and drink.

✉ Between Diagonal Street and Oriental Plaza

Market Theatre

✉ Bree Street, New Town ☎ 011-832 1641; www.markettheatre.co.za

Parktown

Developed on a hillside away from the city centre, this was Johannesburg's first garden suburb. Many gracious stone mansions were built here, several designed by Sir Herbert Baker, South Africa's best-known architect. Over recent decades office development has encroached alarmingly, but a number of the original houses remain. Baker's own home, Stone Cottage, survives, as does Moot Cottage, where Lord Alfred Milner met with his group of young imperial administrators, the so-called Kindergarten, around 1900.

www.parktownheritage.co.za

🛈 Parktown and Westcliff Heritage Trust
✉ 21 Rockridge Road ☎ 011-482 3349
(also fax). Phones/fax staffed weekdays 9–1

Randburg Waterfront

Cape Town started the trend and Johannesburg has followed with its very own – also extremely popular – waterfront development. This one is built around the shores of an artificial lake, fed by the Jukskei River. Shoppers have the choice of a large number of retail outlets, as well as the Harbour Flea Market with some 360 stalls. More than 50 restaurants and pubs offer a great variety of options for eating and drinking. In addition there are 10 cinemas, fountains, watersports, a climbing wall, bungee jumping, a range where you can chip golf balls on to a floating island green, and a large entertainment complex for children.

www.rwaterfront.co.za

✉ Republic Road, Ferndale, Randburg, north Johannesburg ☎ 011-789 5052
🕓 Daily 10 until late

South African National Museum of Military History

Set on the edge of the fine gardens containing the Johannesburg Zoo (▶ 147), this highly rated museum is dedicated to the history of South Africa at war. Objects from World Wars I and II include displays of aircraft, artillery and tanks. A notable exhibit is a German one-man submarine. There are also collections of swords, guns, medals, flags, uniforms and documents relating to war.

www.militarymuseum.co.za

✉ 20 Erlswold Way, Saxonwold ☎ 011-646 5513 🕐 Daily 9–4:30
✋ Free

Soweto

Despite its African sounding name, Soweto is actually an acronym for 'South Western Townships'. Like all the other so-called 'townships' of South Africa, it was the product of the policies of racial segregation of successive white governments. The township began life in 1944 as a residential area for blacks, located some 20km (12.5 miles) southwest of the white suburbs of Johannesburg. Soweto expanded in the 1950s, when many thousands of box-like, tin-roofed houses were built. The famous Soweto Uprising of 1976, started by schoolchildren protesting against Afrikaans as a compulsory subject, spelled the beginning of the end for white rule in South Africa. Today Soweto is a teeming, vibrant, often dangerous place: a mixture of shanties, vast expanses of tiny houses and upscale residential areas. Tourists should visit only with people who know the area, or as part of an organized tour.

www.soweto.co.za

✚ 20J

Jimmy's Face to Face Tours

✚ 130 Main Street, City Centre ☎ 011-331 6109; www.face2face.co.za
✋ Moderate ❓ Variety of tours offered, with or without meal; also night tours

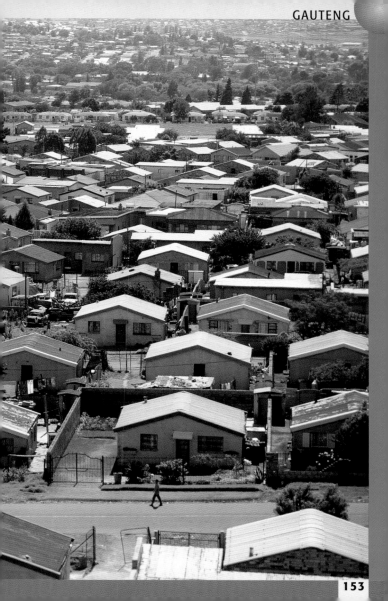

a drive to the Magaliesberg

This drive takes you out of the urban sprawl of Gauteng to the low mountain range of the Magaliesberg.

Take the R511 north from Johannesburg, between Randburg and Sandton. After about 30km (18.5 miles) turn on to the N4 and head northwest in the direction of Rustenburg. You will soon reach the Magaliesberg at Hartbeespoort Dam. (From Pretoria you can reach the same point by taking the N4 west.)

Hartbeespoort Dam is a popular local resort offering fishing, water sports, birdwatching and restaurants. (If you wish to go down to the water take the turn-off to Kosmos.)

Continue west on the N4 to Rustenburg.

All along this stretch you will see the Magaliesberg Nature Reserve, with the low ridge of the mountains on your left.

Just before Rustenburg turn left on to the R24/R30 and head south. After passing over the mountain at Olifantsnek, turn left on to the R24 to Maanhaarrand.

Maanhaarrand ('ridge with a mane') is famous for its many prehistoric rock engravings.

Continue southeast from Maanhaarrand on the R24 for just over 8km (5 miles), then turn left on to the R560 in the direction of Hekpoort.

Just to the north of Hekpoort the Boers defeated a large British contingent at the Battle of Nooitgedacht in December 1900, during the Anglo-Boer War.

From Hekpoort continue northeast along the R560 for 21.5km (13 miles), then turn right on to the R512 which returns to Johannesburg. (If returning to Pretoria, stay on the R560, which will take you to the N4 back to Pretoria.)

Distance From Johannesburg 250km (155 miles); from Pretoria 200km (124 miles)
Time From Johannesburg, 4 hours without stops, 6 hours with stops; from Pretoria, 3.5 hours without stops, 5.5 hours with stops
Start/end point North Johannesburg, Randburg/Sandton area; or central Pretoria
Lunch or tea Mount Grace Hotel (££)
✉ 2.4km (1.5 miles) from Magaliesburg ☎ 014-577 1350

PRETORIA (TSHWANE)

Somewhat more subdued than its southerly neighbour
Johannesburg, Pretoria was founded in the mid-19th century as
capital of the Boers' Transvaal Republic, but was occupied by
British forces during the Anglo-Boer War. In 1910, Pretoria was
chosen as the administrative capital of the newly formed Union of
South Africa, a role it retains in the modern republic. In 2000, the
name of the municipality in which the city lies was changed to
Tshwane (meaning 'Place of the Black Cow', in reference to the
use of this beast in a local rainmaking ritual) and it is possible that
Pretoria will soon adopt this name too. With its compact grid-like
centre of stately Victorian buildings and jacaranda-lined streets,
Pretoria makes for a relaxed alternative base to Johannesburg, and
is probably safer too, though a degree of vigilance is advised.

✚ 20K ✉ Gauteng

African Window

This innovative complex brings together items selected from many
Pretoria museums to give an overview of the different cultures of
South Africa. Clothing, toys, jewellery and objects of archaeological
and anthropological interest are on display. A special exhibit

highlights the lifestyle of the Hananwa people of the Blue Mountains, and there are examples of Bushman rock art, as well as live demonstrations of traditional cooking, music and dance.

✉ 149 Visagie Street ☎ 012-324 6082 ⏰ Daily 8–4 🖐 Inexpensive
🍴 Restaurant (££)

Melrose House

This strange house, with its two odd gables, deep veranda and elaborate ironwork, was built by George Heys, a successful stage-coach operator in 1886. Its wallpapered rooms, paintings and heavy furniture give a vivid idea of the way of life of a wealthy businessman in the Transvaal of the 19th century. A stained-glass window depicts Sir Walter Scott's *Lay of the Last Minstrel*. The Treaty of Vereeniging that ended the Anglo-Boer War was signed in the dining room on 31 May 1902.

www.melrosehouse.co.za

✉ 275 Jacob Mare Street ☎ 012-322 2805 ⏰ Tue–Sun 10–5 🖐 Inexpensive

National Zoological Gardens

Generally rated the best in South Africa, Pretoria's zoo is set in beautiful gardens, with an ornate Victorian fountain. A highlight is the zoo's cableway, giving passengers a bird's-eye view of the gardens. On the ground you can see several thousand animals, numbering around 120 species, housed in good re-creations of natural settings. Among them are most of South Africa's major species, including rarities such as the brown hyena and pigmy hippo, as well as bears, tapirs and apes from other countries.

✉ 232 Boom Street ☎ 012-328 3265 🕐 Daily 8–5 ✋ Moderate
🍴 Restaurant (££), kiosk (£)

Paul Kruger House Museum

Paul Kruger, arguably the most famous Afrikaner, was President of the Transvaal Republic from 1883 to 1900, though he is better known today for initiating the creation of the national park that now bears his name. The plain, twin-gabled house in which he lived throughout that period is now a museum. On display are his desk, a collection of his pipes, a flag of the old Republic and one of the first telephones to be installed in Pretoria. A particularly gruesome exhibit is the knife Kruger used to amputate his thumb after a hunting accident. Outside are his private and state rail coaches.

✉ 60 Church Street ☎ 012-326 9172 🕐 Tue–Sat 8:30–4, Sun 11–4
✋ Inexpensive

Transvaal Museum

For bird-lovers this museum, focusing mainly on natural history, is not to be missed. In the Austin Roberts Bird Hall, named after the author of the first ornithological field guide to the region, you will find a comprehensive display of stuffed birds of Southern Africa, and can listen to the recorded call of most species. Elsewhere are a dodo skeleton and mammal and reptile galleries.

✉ 432 Paul Kruger Street ☎ 012-322 7632 🕐 Mon–Sat 9–5, Sun and public holidays 11–5 ✋ Inexpensive 🍴 Restaurant (££)

Union Buildings

The Union Buildings are the masterpiece of architect Sir Herbert Baker. The majestic structure, with its two wings, each with its own tower, and linked by a graceful colonnaded amphitheatre, was built to mark the formation of the Union of South Africa in 1910. It has been the seat of the executive of successive governments, most recently that of the post-1994 ANC government. The amphitheatre has witnessed many historic events; a funeral service was held here in 1966 for Hendrik Verwoerd, the architect of apartheid, and the country's most recent presidents, Nelson Mandela and Thabo Mbeki, were sworn in here.

✉ Government Avenue ☎ 012-300 5200 ⏏ No access to inside of buildings; ask police on duty for permission to view outside

Voortrekker Monument and Museum

This monument to the outdated ideology of Afrikaner nationalism remains strangely moving. The massive granite edifice, 40m (131ft) high and set on an imposing base, was opened in December 1949. The outside of the building bristles with symbols: a wall of ox-wagons, a barrier of Zulu spears, reliefs of wild animals, busts of Voortrekker leaders, a statue of a Voortrekker woman and children. The most striking feature of the interior is the monumental marble frieze, 92m (300ft) long, showing the Great Trek, in which Afrikaner pioneers journeyed to the interior of South Africa. Although its generally demeaning portrayal of blacks is offensive, the frieze is a powerful piece of work. In the nearby museum, tapestries depicting the Great Trek, and Voortrekker possessions and weapons are on display.

www.voortrekkermon.org.za

✉ Monument Hill, 6km from city centre ☎ 012-326 6770 🕐 Daily 8–5
✋ Moderate 🍴 Restaurant (££), kiosk (£) ❓ Phone for guided tours

HOTELS

JOHANNESBURG
Airport Grand Hotel (££)
Good value hotel for short stopovers, with regular airport shuttles and conveniently located opposite East Rand Mall.

✉ 100 North Rand Road, 5–10 minutes from OR Tambo Airport, Johannesburg, Gauteng ☎ 011-823 1843; www.legacyhotels.co.za

Garden Court Hotel (££–£££)
Siutated in stylish Sandton, north of the city centre. Luxurious, but not exorbitantly priced. Pleasant à la carte restaurant and bar. On-site pool and close to the excellent Sandton City shopping mall.

✉ 15 Katherine Street, Sandown, Johannesburg, Gauteng ☎ 011-884 854; www.southernsun.com

The Grace (£££)
This is a very stylish upscale hotel set in an opulent mansion in trendy Rosebank, and offers the combination of excellent facilities and access to the city's top restaurants and shops.

✉ 54 Bath Avenue, Rosebank, Johannesburg, Gauteng ☎ 011-780 7200; www.grace.co.za.

The Melville Turret Guest House (£–££)
Set in a beautiful, turreted old house in a quiet suburb. Near to popular 7th Street and its restaurants, nightclubs and cafés.

✉ 118 2nd Avenue (corner with 9th Street), Melville, Johannesburg, Gauteng ☎ 011-482 7197

Park Hyatt (£££)
In the fashionable suburb of Rosebank. Cocktail terrace, excellent restaurant. Wine bar features nightly live music.

✉ 191 Oxford Road, Rosebank, Johannesburg, Gauteng ☎ 011-280 1234; www.johannesburg.park.hyatt.com

PRETORIA
Garden Court Pretoria (££)
Comfortable, centrally situated former Holiday Inn, within walking

distance of the main attractions. Restaurants.

✉ Corner of End and Pretorius streets, Hatfield, Pretoria, Gauteng

☎ 012-342 1444; www.southernsun.com

Park Gables (£–££)

Small guest house with spacious rooms near Pretoria Art Museum.

✚ 784 Park Street, Arcadia, Pretoria, Gauteng ✉ 012-325 7570;
www.parkgables.co.za

Pretoria Hof Hotel (££)

Right in the heart of the city, next to the State Theatre, this hotel offers comfort at reasonable rates; restaurant.

✉ 295 Pretorius Street, Pretoria, Gauteng ☎ 012-325 7570

Sheraton Pretoria (£££)

Pretoria's only five-star accommodation is also probably its largest hotel, with excellent facilities and a convenient near-central location overlooking the Union Buildings.

✉ Corner of Church and Wessels, Arcadia, Pretoria, Gauteng ☎ 012-429 9999; www.starwoodhotels.com

RESTAURANTS

JOHANNESBURG
Bukhara Restaurant (£££)

Recently opened Johannesburg branch of Cape Town's leading North Indian restaurant.

✉ Sandton Square, 5th Street, Sandton, Johannesburg, Gauteng

☎ 011-833 5555

Le Canard (££)

Offers a choice of eating indoors or on the terrace. Try the delicious sauces with duck, seafood or venison. Good range of wines.

✉ 163 Rivonia Road, Morningside, Sandton, Johannesburg, Gauteng

☎ 011-884 4597 ⏰ Mon–Fri lunch; Mon–Sat dinner

The Carnivore (£££)

Situated in Midrand, towards Pretoria, this branch of its legendary

Nairobi namesake serves an all-you-can-eat buffet, including several types of venison and the likes of crocodile and zebra!

✉ 69 Drift Road, Muldersdrift, Johannesburg, Gauteng ☎ 011-957 3132

Chez Girard (£££)

Chic but unpretentious French restaurant serving fine Burgundian cuisine. Sample the salmon quenelles with brandy sauce.

✉ 1 Cullinan Close, Morningside, Johannesburg, Gauteng ☎ 011-784 2105
🕐 Mon–Fri lunch; Mon–Sat dinner

Cranks (££)

This is an excellent, sensibly priced and funky Thai restaurant in Rosebank Mall.

✉ Rosebank Mall, Rosebank, Johannesburg, Gauteng ☎ 011-880 3442

Gramadoelas (££)

Interesting eclectic African décor. The restaurant specializes in South African cuisine, particularly Cape Malay. Traditional fare such as mopani worms and crocodile also on offer.

✉ Market Theatre Complex, Johannesburg, Gauteng ☎ 011-838 6960; www.gramadoelas.co.za 🕐 Tue–Sat lunch; Tue–Sun dinner

Linger Longer (£££)

Something of a Johannesburg institution, this French restaurant is known for its gourmet dishes, classical décor and wine list.

✉ 58 Wierda Valley Road, Johannesburg, Gauteng ☎ 011-884 0465

Moyo (£££)

A great place for foreigners to visit, this venue offers Pan-African food and culture. The food leans towards North Africa, with many Moroccan specialties, such as *harira* (a peppery soup).

✉ Melrose Square, Melrose Arch, Johannesburg, Gauteng ☎ 011-684 1477; www.moyo.co.za 🕐 Daily lunch and dinner

Wandies Place

This cosy and casual pub and eatery in Soweto was one of the first to open to post-apartheid tourism. It has hosted the likes of

Richard Branson, Brad Pitt, Jesse Jackson and the All Blacks.
✉ Makhalamele Street, Soweto, Gauteng ☎ 011-326 1700;
www.wandies.co.za 🕐 Times vary

PRETORIA
Brasserie de Paris (££)
Serving beautifully presented French food in an intimate
atmosphere, this brasserie has a varied menu, including pork fillet
with prunes and roast guineafowl, and a well-selected wine list.
✉ 381 Aries Street Waterkloof Ridge, Pretoria, Gauteng ☎ 012-460 3583
🕐 Mon–Fri lunch; Mon–Sat dinner

Die Werf (££)
Offering local dishes and a choice of unusual specialties such as
curried mutton tripe in a country house setting.
✉ Plot 66, Olympus Road, Faerie Glen, Pretoria, Gauteng ☎ 012-991 1809
🕐 Tue–Sun lunch; Tue–Sat dinner

Pachas (££)
Bright interior, wall-papered with menus. Interesting mix of dishes,
such as smoked duck breast, lobster bisque and ostrich kebabs.
✉ Club II Shopping Centre, 22 Dely Road, Hazelwood, Pretoria, Gauteng
☎ 012-460 5063 🕐 Sun–Fri lunch; Mon–Sat dinner

SHOPPING

Bruma Lake Flea Market
Located near Eastgate Shopping Mall, hundreds of stalls sell crafts
from all over Africa, as well as everything from clothing to food.
✉ Marcia St, Bruma, Johannesburg, Gauteng ☎ 011-622 9648
🕐 Tue–Sun 9:30–5

Mukondeni Art Gallery
Sells South African sculpture, pottery and art of outstanding quality
✉ 36 Orleans Road, Kya Sands, Johannesburg, Gauteng ☎ 011-708 2116

Africa Craft Market and Rooftop Market
Excellent African craft market, boosted by popular Sunday rooftop

market with secondhand goods, antiques and live entertainment.

✉ Rosebank Mall, Johannesburg, Gauteng ☎ 011-880 2096 (craft market) 011-442 4488 (rooftop) 🕐 Craft market: daily; rooftop: Sun only

Eastgate Shopping Mall

This is one of the largest malls on the continent. Includes a range of department stores, boutiques and entertainment facilities.

✉ 43 Bradford Road, Bedford View, Johannesburg, Gauteng ☎ 011-616 2209; www.eastgatecentre.co.za

Oriental Plaza

Indian-dominated mall especially strong on spices and fabrics.

✉ Main and Avenue streets, Fordsburg, Johannesburg, Gauteng
☎ 011-838 6752

Rosebank Mall & The Zone@Rosebank

Facing each other in trendy Rosebank, both malls have a large range shops. The former hosts the country's leading 'art' cinema.

✉ Jan Smuts Avenue, Rosebank, Johannesburg, Gauteng ☎ 011-788 5530; www.mallofrosebank.co.za

Randburg Waterfront

See page 151.

ENTERTAINMENT

Café Barcelona

Live bands play their blues, jazz and rock compositions at this restaurant/bar.

✚ Elardus Park Shopping Centre, Barnard Street, Pretoria, Gauteng
✉ 012-345 3606 ☎ Mon–Sat noon–2am

Roxy Rhythm Bar

Now almost 20 years old, this live music spot hosts original acts almost every night of the week; occasional DJs.

✉ Corner of Main Road and 5th Avenue, Melville, Johannesburg, Gauteng
☎ 011-726 6019 🕐 Mon–Sat 8pm–late

Northwest Region

Kimberley

This vast, thinly populated area, mountainous in the east, includes rolling prairie, maize fields, Karoo scrub and semi-desert. Small numbers of Bushmen still live here, descendants of the bands of hunter-gatherers who used to roam these arid expanses.

The economy of the region relies on agriculture, sustained in many places by irrigation from the Vaal and Gariep (formerly Orange) rivers, and on the mining of diamonds around Kimberley and gold in the Free State. With the growth of tourism in South Africa, many farmers have turned to game farming to attract commercial hunters to the area.

Visitors come to the region for the fine game reserves, the spring flowers of the Northern Cape, and for peace and quiet. The more active will find rafting and canoeing on the Gariep River, many recently opened 4x4 trails, and a variety of hiking trails through rugged, sun-scorched landscapes.

KIMBERLEY

The history of Kimberley, capital of the
Northern Cape, is inseparable from the
story of diamond mining in South
Africa. The fabulous treasure-house of
diamonds, the Big Hole, was the centre
from which the city grew. The present
population is about 200,000.

Named after the British Colonial
Secretary of the time, the Earl of
Kimberley, the city was founded in
1871. In 1878, when it was first granted municipal status,
Kimberley was still a rough miners' camp but from then on
things improved rapidly. In 1882 this was the first African city to
get electric street lights, and in 1887 trams started to run.

Two men dominated early Kimberley and the diamond
business. One was Barney Barnato, a former barman, boxer and
music-hall artiste from the East End of London who came to
South Africa in 1873. Starting out as a digger and diamond-
buyer, he became a multimillionaire by the age of 25. Barnato's
great rival was Cecil John Rhodes. The son of an English
clergyman, Rhodes came to South Africa in 1870, at the age of
17, and quickly amassed a fortune. When Rhodes's company
De Beers Consolidated Mines, bought out Barnato in 1888,
De Beers gained a monopoly over the trade in diamonds only
recently relinquished.

During the Anglo-Boer War, the Boers besieged Kimberley
for four months. Famous battles were fought near the city at
Modderrivier and Magersfontein, where trenches were used
for the first time in modern warfare when the Boers dug in
below the hill at Magersfontein.

The diamond mines at Kimberley still produce some 4,000
carats of diamonds a day.

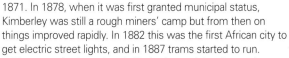 7F Northern Cape

The Big Hole and Kimberley Mine Museum

In 1869 diamonds were discovered at Bultfontein, near the place which grew into the city of Kimberley in the Northern Cape. Two years later the diamond diggers' attention shifted to an insignificant-looking nearby hillock, Colesberg Koppie. Very soon the hill had disappeared into a huge pit.

What the diggers had stumbled on was the mouth of an enormous, ancient volcanic vent filled with a bluish clay-like substance – a so-called kimberlite pipe. This one was extraordinarily rich in diamonds. Over the 43 years that the pipe

ALEXANDERSFONTEIN ELECTRIC RAILWAY

was worked no fewer than 2,720kg (5,984 lb) of diamonds were taken from it. All that was left here when the mining stopped was the Big Hole, 800m (2,624ft) deep. Even today, when it is filled with water to within 174m (570ft) of the top, the Big Hole is an awe-inspiring sight, with a circumference of 1.6km (1 mile), and a surface area that extends over more than 13ha (32 acres).

A tram route runs to the Big Hole from the centre of Kimberley and by the hole's rim you'll find the streets and buildings of the open-air Kimberley Mine Museum. Original offices, private houses, a church, a pub, a pawnbroker's shop, a blacksmith's workshop and Barney Barnato's Boxing Academy can be visited, and photographs portray city life during the diamond rush. In the diamond exhibition hall 2,000 carats of real diamonds are on display, alongside replicas of some the world's most famous gems. Nearby, the 19th-century pub, the Star of the West, offers refreshment.

✉ Tucker Street ☎ 053-833 1557 🕐 Daily 8–5 ✋ Expensive
🍴 Restaurant (£)

Wildebeest Kuil Rock Art Site
Opened to tourism in 2001, this rock art site 15km (10 miles) outside Kimberley contains several thousand-year-old engravings of elephants and other animals, attributed to the Bushmen hunter-gatherers who formerly inhabited much of South Africa. A well-structured tour starts with a 25-minute introductory film then follows a short walking trail to 10 listening posts where insightful audio commentary is provided.

www.museumsnc.co.za/wildebeestkuil.htm

✉ 15km (10 miles) from Kimberly off the Barkley West Road
☎ 053-833 7069 🕐 Tue–Fri 10–5, Sat and Sun 11–4 ✋ Moderate

More to see in the Northwest Region

AUGRABIES FALLS NATIONAL PARK

At the heart of this 28,000ha (69,160 acre) park lie the Augrabies Falls – the name means 'place of the great noise' in the Khoikhoi language. Here, the Gariep River, South Africa's largest, plunges 65m (213ft) into a granite funnel and a deep, narrow ravine that runs for 18km (11 miles) below the falls. The park offers standard game drives (common wildlife includes springbok, klipspringer and – on the north side of the river – black rhino) and night drives that offer the opportunity to see nocturnal predators such as African

wild cat, bat-eared fox, brown hyena and aardwolf. An easy day trail and more demanding three-day hiking trail run through this rocky, moonlike landscape, set with beautiful, branching kokerbooms (quiver trees).
www.sanparks.org

✚ 14G ✉ 120km (75 miles) west of Upington, Northern Cape

☎ Park: 054-451 0050; reservations: 012-428 9111 ⊘ Daily 24 hours
✋ Moderate 🍴 Restaurant (££)

BLOEMFONTEIN

Also known as Mangaung, Bloemfontein ('Spring of Flowers') was originally the capital of the former Boer Republic of the Orange Free State. At the formation of the Union in 1910 the city became the seat of the Appeal Court and judicial capital of South Africa, which it remains to this day. The historic city centre around President Brand Street features the simple, thatched First Raadsaal (council chamber) with mud and dung floor, the more elaborate Fourth Raadsaal, and the Presidency, official residence of the head of the old republic. Within walking distance are the

Appeal Court and the Queen's Fort of 1848. Highlights of the National Museum are the fossil collection and the re-creation of a 19th-century street. Naval Hill, a small nature reserve right in the centre of Bloemfontein, provides good views over the city.

Not to be missed is the National Women's Memorial and War Museum, showing the horror of the concentration camps in which the British imprisoned civilians during the Anglo-Boer War. More than 40,000 Africans and Afrikaners died in these camps.

www.bloemfontein.co.za

✚ 8E ✉ Free State

ℹ 60 Park Road, Willows ☎ 051-405 8489/90

National Museum

✉ 36 Aliwal Street ☎ 051-447 9609; www.nasmus.co.za 🕐 Mon–Fri 8–5, Sat 10–5, Sun 12–5:30 ✋ Inexpensive 🍴 Restaurant (££)

COLESBERG

This pretty town in the heart of the Karoo is a great place to get away from it all. Motorists often stay overnight here to break their journey between Gauteng and the Western Cape. Founded in 1830, Colesberg still has many of its 19th-century private houses, churches and public buildings. There are several pleasant bed-and-breakfasts and restaurants in the town, as well as a pub in the old mill house.

✚ 7D ✉ Northern Cape
ℹ Museum Square, Murray Street
☎ 051-753 0678

GARIEP DAM

When full, this dam on the Gariep and Caledon rivers, built in the early 1870s, creates a lake that covers 374sq km (146sq miles), South Africa's largest inland body of water. The dam wall is 914m (996 yards) long and extensive tunnels from here feed irrigation systems some distance away. Bordering the dam, the Gariep Nature Reserve is the largest in the Free State.

✚ 8D ✉ 160km (100 miles) south of Bloemfontein, Free State ☎ 051-754 0026/48

GOLDEN GATE HIGHLANDS NATIONAL PARK

The Golden Gate Highlands National Park, so-called for the twin buttresses of golden sandstone that rear up on either side of the park entrance, is the central attraction of the Free State region. In the reserve you can see the native black wildebeest, as well as eland, oribi, red hartebeest and various birds, including the lack eagle and bearded vulture. But it is the landscape, rather than the wildlife, that visitors come to see.

The deep layer of soft sandstone laid down over this region has been weathered by wind and water into fantastic shapes. In many places the red, ochre and gold layers, while protected from above by a cap of harder stone, have been eroded from below to create shadowy overhangs and great mushroom formations.

Nearby is the picturesque town of Clarens (➤ 180), which is increasingly popular with arty refugees from Gauteng and tourists.

www.sanparks.org

✚ 21G ✉ 18km (11 miles) east of Clarens, Free State
☎ 058-255 0012 ⏱ 24 hours daily ✋ Day visitors: inexpensive
🍴 Restaurant and pub (££) ✈ Fly to Bloemfontein
❓ Horse riding, fishing and hiking ☎ 058-256 1189
ℹ Free State Tourist Office ☎ 051-405 8489/90

KGALAGADI TRANSFRONTIER PARK

Kgalagadi was created in 1999 with the fusion of South Africa's Kalahari Gemsbok National Park and Botswana's Gemsbok National Park to create a cross-border park that extends over 3.8 million ha (94 million acres) – almost twice the size of Israel or the Kruger National Park. This vast size allows for a phenomenon once common in Africa: the large-scale nomadic and seasonal movement of animals.

Kgalagadi is unexpectedly scenic, with its tall red dunes, dry acacia-lined riverbeds, and rapturously clear night skies. And despite its aridity and a few notable absentees (for instance elephant, buffalo and giraffe), the wildlife viewing is exceptional – black-maned lions, cheetah and leopard are seen with some frequency, while antelope include springbok, eland and the magnificent spear-horned gemsbok (oryx).

www.sanparks.org

🚻 15K ✉ 216km (130 miles) north of Upington, Northern Cape

☎ Park: 054-561 2000; reservations: 012-428 9111 🕐 Daily 7:30–6:30

✋ Moderate 🍴 Restaurant (££)

NAMAKWA (ALSO NAMAQUA AND NAMAQUALAND)

This area of the Northern Cape, south of the Gariep River, is at its best in spring, when it is transformed into a brilliant carpet of flowers (Best places to see, ➤ 48–49). A good place to see the spring flowers, as well as 94 bird and 45 mammal species, is the Goegap Nature Reserve, 15km (9 miles) east of the region's main town of Springbok, a growing centre for outdoor activities. In the

extreme northwest of Namaqualand, accessible by 4x4 only, the starkly beautiful mountains of Richtersveld National Park host an astonishing variety of desert-adapted mammals, reptiles, birds and plants, including the tall succulent *Pachypodium namaquanum*, better known as the 'halfmensboom' (half human tree) on account of its strange bulbous silhouette.

➕ 2D ✉ Northern Cape

ℹ Voortrekker Street, Springbok ☎ 027-712 2011; www.northerncape.org.za

🕓 Mon–Fri 7:30–4:15 and (flower season only, ➤ 48–49; Sat–Sun 9–12)

UPINGTON

Police mounted on camels used to operate out of Upington, the main town on the Gariep River and best springboard for visits to Kgalagadi. Unlikely as it may seem in this semi-desert region, the town is now a centre for grape growing due to extensive irrigation from the river. The grapes are used mainly for raisins but wine is also produced by the Orange River Wine Co-operative.

A number of companies use Upington as a base for canoeing and river-rafting safaris on the Gariep. Worth a visit are Olyvenhout Island, with its avenue of date palms, and the nearby **Spitskop Game Reserve,** which hosts similar species to Kgalagadi.

www.upington.com

➕ 15H ✉ Northern Cape

ℹ Schröder Street ☎ 054-332 6064 🕓 Mon–Fri 8–5:30, Sat 9–12

Spitskop Game Reserve

✉ 13km (8 miles) northwest of Upington ☎ 054-332 1336; www.spitskopmonate.com

PILANESBERG NATIONAL PARK

Lake Mankwe, in the crater of an extinct volcano, lies at the centre of this 55,000ha (136,000-acre) park. A number of local farmers were displaced to create the reserve in the 1970s and a massive programme of relocation of animals was undertaken. The Big Five can now be seen here, as are more than 300 species of bird, many types of antelope, giraffe, zebra and hippo. Because the park lies in a transitional ecological zone, springbok and impala can, very unusually, be seen together here. The low-set hides near water-holes make for excellent game viewing. Hot-air balloon trips over the reserve are available. This park is close to Johannesburg and Pretoria, making it ideal for a short break.

www.pilanesberg-game-reserve.co.za

➕ 20K ✉ 190km (118 miles) northwest of Johannesburg, Northwest Province ☎ 14-555 5354 🕐 Daily 6:30–6 ✋ Moderate 🍴 Snack bar (£)

SUN CITY

Some two hours' drive northwest of Johannesburg lies the entertainment and holiday resort of Sun City. Connoisseurs of kitsch will love this place, which actually consists of two parts: the newer Lost City, and the older Sun City.

The Lost City follows a theme, attempting to re-create *King Solomon's Mines*, a novel by the colonial writer H Rider Haggard. At the two 'Cities' you will find an artificial beach, complete with artificial surf, a casino, American-style showgirl-extravaganzas, golf courses with real crocodiles in the water hazard, playgrounds and a petting zoo for the children. If you need to get back to nature, the Pilanesberg National Park (➤ opposite) is right next door.

www.suninternational.com/resorts/suncity

✚ 20K ✉ 190km (118 miles) northwest of Johannesburg, Northwest Province ☎ 014-557 1000 ⏰ Daily 8:30–5 🍴 Many outlets (£–£££)

a drive along the Eastern Highlands of the Free State

This drive takes you through superb countryside alongside South Africa's border with Lesotho.

Take the R712 from Golden Gate Highlands National Park (▶ 175) to the town of Clarens, 18km (11 miles) away.

Clarens, named after the Swiss resort where President Paul Kruger died in 1904, is beautifully situated below golden sandstone cliffs. Many artists have come to live here, and the town has restaurants, gift shops and a very good book shop.

From Clarens drive southwest on the R711. After 36km (22 miles) reach Fouriesburg.

The road passes by picturesque sandstone outcrops, forming low flat-topped hills. All along this stretch to your left are Lesotho's Maloti Mountains, often capped with snow in winter. Look out for signs directing you to the many Bushman rock paintings in the area. Fouriesburg, founded in 1892, was the seat of the Orange Free State government for a time during the Anglo-Boer War. Excellent meals can be had at the Fouriesburg Country Inn.

Just after Fouriesburg is a T-junction. Turn left here on to the R26 in the direction of Ficksburg, 56km (35 miles) away.

The town of Ficksburg, situated 5km (3 miles) from a major entry point into Lesotho, is very much a border town, with hundreds of people coming in every day from Lesotho to shop. A Cherry Festival and a Vintage Tractor Show are held here annually (➤ 24–25).

From Ficksburg, if you have the time, you can continue southwest on the R26 to the town of Clocolan. Return to Golden Gate along the same route.

Distance 220km/136 miles (290km/180 miles if you go on to Clocolan)
Time 3 hours without stops; 6 hours with stops
Start/end point Golden Gate Highlands National Park ✚ 21G
Tea or Lunch Fouriesburg Country Inn (£–££) ✉ Reitz Street ☎ 058-223 0207

HOTELS

BLOEMFONTEIN
De Oude Kraal Country Estate (££)
Relax under the blue gums on this farm just outside Bloemfontein. Has traditional farm cooking, its own pub, comfortable accommodation, swimming and riding.

✉ Tierpoort, 35km (22 miles) south of Bloemfontein, Free State ☎ 051-564 0636; www.oudekraal.co.za

Protea Hotel Bloemfontein (££)
Has the inevitable sameness of a chain hotel, but with the advantage of being centrally situated, near historic sights.

✉ 202 Nelson Mandela Drive, Bloemfontein, Free State ☎ 051-444 4321; www.proteahotels.co.za

LADYBRAND
Cranberry Cottage (££)
Antique-filled guest house; pretty garden. Ideal base to visit Lesotho and the many prehistoric rock paintings in the area.

✉ 37 Beeton Street, Ladybrand, Free State ☎ 051-924 2290; www.cranberrycottages.co.za

NORTHWEST PROVINCE
Sun City (££–£££)
See pages 178–179.

Bakubung (£££)
Located in the Pilanesberg Game Reserve (► 178), this resort offers luxurious rooms with views of the bushveld and a waterhole with resident hippo, outdoor barbecues, a natural rock swimming pool and day and night drives.

✉ Pilanesberg Game Reserve 0300, Northwest Province ☎ 014-552 6000; www.legacyhotels.co.za

KIMBERLEY
Protea Hotel Diamond Lodge (££)
In central Kimberley, just five minutes from the Big Hole

(➤ 169–170). Comfortable, centrally heated rooms; a variety of restaurants nearby.

✉ 124 Du Toitspan Road, Kimberley, Northern Cape ☎ 053-831 1281; www.proteahotels.co.za

OKIEP
Okiep Country Hotel (££)

This comfortable and modestly priced country hotel, just 10 minutes' drive from central Springbok, is an ideal base for viewing the spectacular spring flowers (➤ 48–49). Owner can advise about 4x4 and hiking trails. Tours offered.

✉ Concordia Rd, Okiep, Northern Cape ☎ 027-744 1000; www.okiep.co.za

UPINGTON
Le Must River Residence (££)

This stylish three-star guesthouse is the undisputed gem of Upington's accommodation scene, and fantastic value too, with friendly service and a lovely setting overlooking the Gariep River.

✉ 14 Butler Street, Upington, Northern Cape ☎ 054 332 3971; www.lemustupington.com

Protea Oasis Lodge (££)

Recently renovated hotel with tropical plants, now the most stylish conventional hotel in Upington. The rooms are comfortable and reasonably priced. Hotel has an in-house bar.

✉ 26 Schröder Street, Upington, Northern Cape ☎ 054-337 8500; www.proteahotels.co.za

RESTAURANTS

BETHLEHEM
The Wooden Spoon (£–££)

Housed in the oldest building in town, this restaurant and pub offers simple, good quality food: *biltong* (dried meat) salad, pork dishes, seafood, and delicious home-made bread.

✉ 12 Church Street, Bethleham, Free State ☎ 058-303 2724 ⊙ Daily breakfast, dinner; Mon–Sat lunch

BLOEMFONTEIN
Beef Baron (££)
Steakhouse with steaks served with an interesting range of sauces – bone marrow and bacon, or spinach and feta cheese. Seafood also available. Comprehensive wine list.

✉ 22 Second Avenue, Westdene, Bloemfontein, Free State ☎ 051-447 4290 🕐 Lunch Tue–Sun; dinner Mon–Sat

Catch 22 (££)
One of the best restaurants locally, it specializes in seafood, but also offers some meat dishes. Try the sole layered with mushrooms, calamari, shrimps and mussels in creamy sauce.

✉ Shop 30A, Upper Level, Mimosa Mall, Bloemfontein, Free State ☎ 051-444 6877 🕐 Lunch, dinner daily

Onze Rust (£££)
Restaurant situated on an old family farm, offering traditional Afrikaner food prepared to a high standard, using the freshest local ingredients. The historic bar has Boer War memorabilia.

✉ 15km (9 miles) south of Bloemfontein, off the N1, Free State ☎ 051-443 8717 🕐 Daily by reservation only

LADYBRAND
Cranberry Cottage (£–££)
Set in a traditional Free State sandstone house, the restaurant offers a set menu with a choice for each course. Delicious, unpretentious food and good value for money.

✉ 37 Beeton Street, Ladybrand, Free State ☎ 051-924 2290 🕐 Daily breakfast, teas, dinner

WELKOM
Siete's Restaurant (££)
Well-established restaurant, serving mainly meat and seafood dishes, with some vegetarian options. Try the blackened Cajun chicken, or flamed pork fillet with spinach and feta.

✉ Adami House 17 Mooi Street, Welkom, Free State ☎ 057-352 6539 🕐 Tue–Fri lunch; Mon–Sat dinner

UPINGTON, NORTHERN CAPE
Le Must Country Restaurant (££)
Winner of numerous awards, Le Must is the best restaurant in town, serving good local dishes (the speciality being Karoo lamb) and international cuisine accompanied by excellent service.

✉ 11 Schröder Street, Upington, Northern Cape ☎ 054-332 3971
🕒 Sun–Fri lunch; daily dinner

SHOPPING

Mimosa Mall
The largest mall in the Free State, with a great selection of restaurants, book and clothing shops and national chain stores.

✉ Dan Pienaar Rd, Bloemfontein, Free State ☎ www.mimosamall.co.za

Orange River Wine Cellars
Try the produce of South Africa's largest wine co-operative, whose ever-improving range of affordable reds and whites is made from grapes grown along the irrigated banks of the Gariep River.

✉ Tasting rooms in Upington, Keimos and Kakamas, Northern Cape
☎ 054-337 8800; www.oranjerivier.com 🕒 Mon–Fri 8–5; Sat 8:30–12

ENTERTAINMENT

Bloemfontein Civic Theatre
The auditorium seats 450 and is used primarily for drama productions.

✉ Markgraf Street, Bloemfontein, Free State ☎ 051-447 7771

Sand du Plessis Theatre
This 960-seat auditorium hosts regular dramas and other shows by the Performing Arts Centre of the Free State (PACOFS).

✉ St Andrews Street, Bloemfontein, Free State ☎ 051-447 7772;
www.pacofs.co.za

Kimberley Theatre
Kimberley's only theatre used as a cinema but also hosts plays.

✉ Kimberley, Northern Cape ☎ 053-831 1761

Index

Acknowledgements

The Automobile Association wishes to thank the following photographers for their assistance in the preparation of this book.

Abbreviations for the picture credits are as follows – (t) top; (b) bottom; (l) left; (r) right; (c) centre; (AA) AA World Travel Library

4l Coastal view, Wilderness, AA/C Sawyer; **4c** Venda, AA/S McBride; **4r** Kruger National Park, AA/S McBride; **5l** Golden Gate Highlands National Park, AA/S McBride; **5c** Table Mountain, AA/C Sawyer; **6/7** Coastal view, Wilderness, AA/C Sawyer; **8/9** Mantenga Cultural Village, AA/S McBride; **10tr** Flowers, uKhahlamba-Drakensberg Mountains, AA/P Kenward; **10/11c** Tea plantation, Magoebaskloof, AA/S McBride; **10/11c** Craft shop, Malkerns Valley, AA/S McBride; **10bl** Zebra, AA/S McBride; **10br** Port Elizabeth, AA/C Sawyer; **11tl** Surfers, Muizenberg, AA/C Sawyer; **11bl** Waterfall, Meiringspoort, AA/C Sawyer; **12/13t** Food selection, AA/Human & Rousseau (Pty) Ltd; **12bl** Bakery, Johannesburg, AA/S McBride; **12/13b** Café, Cape Town, AA/C Sawyer; **13tr** Plate of food, AA/Human & Rousseau (Pty) Ltd; **14tl** Restaurant, Durban, AA/S McBride; **14/15t** Pancake, AA/S McBride; **14cl** Tomato Bredie, AA/Human & Rousseau (Pty) Ltd; **14bl** Fish Shop, AA/C Sawyer; **14/15b** Wine, AA/C Sawyer; **15tr** Sign, AA/C Sawyer; **15br** Oysters and Wine, AA/C Sawyer; **16/17t** Central Beach View,

Plettenberg, AA/C Sawyer; **16/17b** Burchell's zebra, Hluhluwe-Imfolozi Game Reserve, AA/C Sawyer; **17tr** Paintings for sale, East London, AA/C Sawyer; **17br** Soweto, AA/C Sawyer; **18t** Cooking pots, AA/C Sawyer; **18b** Outdoor meal, Shamwari Game Reserve, AA/C Sawyer; **19t** Gariep Dam, AA/S McBride; **19c** Wine Cellar, Franschhoek AA/C Sawyer; **19b** Wine Tasting, Franschhoek, AA/C Sawyer; **20/21** Dirt road, Venda, AA/S McBride; **25** Fisherman Painting Boat, Arniston, AA/C Sawyer; **34/35** Kruger National Park, AA/S McBride; **36cl** Bourke's Luck Potholes, Blyde River Canyon, AA/S McBride; **36/37** Lisbon Falls, Blyde River Canyon, AA/S McBride; **37tr** Three Rondavels, Blyde River Canyon, AA/S McBride; **37br** Echo Caves, Blyde River Canyon, AA/S McBride; **38/39t** Clifton Beach, Cape Town, AA/C Sawyer; **38/39b** View from Signal Hill, Cape Town, AA/C Sawyer; **40/41** Sterkfontein Caves, South African Tourism; **42/43** Tsitsikamma National Park, AA/C Sawyer; **43tr** Seal Island, Mossel Bay, AA/C Sawyer; **44/45t** Hippo's, Greater St Lucia Wetland Park, AA/S McBride; **44/45c** Tour group, AA/S McBride; **44b** Bird of prey, Greater St Lucia Wetland Park, AA/S McBride; **46/47t** Elephant, Kruger National Park, AA/S McBride; **46/47b** Baobab tree, Kruger National Park, AA/S McBride; **48/49t** Quiver Trees, Namaqualand, South African Tourism; **48/49b** Namaqualand Daisies, Goegap Nature Reserve, South African Tourism; **49br** Halfmens, Richtersveld, South African Tourism; **50/51t** Prison, Robben Island, AA/C Sawyer; **50l** Prison, Robben Island, AA/C Sawyer; **50/51b** Table Mountain from Robben Island, AA/C Sawyer; **52/53t** Waterfall, Drakensberg, AA/P Kenward; **52/53b** Drakensberg, AA/P Kenward; **54cl** Clock tower, Victoria and Alfred Waterfront, AA/C Sawyer; **54/55b** Victoria and Alfred Waterfront, AA/C Sawyer; **55t** Victoria and Alfred Waterfront, AA/C Sawyer; **56/57** Golden Gate Highlands National Park, AA/S McBride; **58/59** Kimberley, AA/C Sawyer; **60/61** Muizenberg, AA/C Sawyer; **62** Aquarium, Cape Town, AA/C Sawyer; **65** Augrabies Falls National Park, AA/C Sawyer; **66/67** Table Mountain seen from Bloubergstrand, AA/C Sawyer; **68** City Hall, Cape Town, AA/C Sawyer; **69tr** Long Street Buildings, Cape Town, AA/C Sawyer; **69b** Company's Garden, Cape Town, AA/C Sawyer; **70** Argus Cycle Race, South African Tourism; **71** Springbok rugby team supporters, South African Tourism; **72/73** View of Table Mountain from Bloubergstrand, AA/C Sawyer; **75** Clifton Beach, Cape Town, AA/C Sawyer; **76/77b** Dining room, Bertram House, AA/C Sawyer; **77t** Exterior, Bertram House, AA/C Sawyer; **78t** Bo-Kaap, AA/C Sawyer; **78bc** Guard, Castle of Good Hope, AA/C Sawyer; **78/79c** Company's Garden, AA/C Sawyer; **80** Greenmarket Square, AA/C Sawyer; **81** District Six Museum, AA/C Sawyer; **82tl** Houses of Parliament, AA/C Sawyer; **82b** Café, Long Town, AA/C Sawyer; **82/83t** Long Street, AA/C Sawyer; **84/85** St George's Cathedral, AA/C Sawyer; **85cr** Slave Lodge, AA/P Kenward; **86/87t** South Africa Museum and Planetarium, AA/C Sawyer; **86b** Dinosaur skeleton, South Africa Museum, AA/C Sawyer; **87bl** South Africa National gallery, AA/C Sawyer; **88tl** Table Mountain Cableway, AA/C Sawyer; **89** Walkers on Table Mountain, AA/C Sawyer; **92t** Addo Elephant National Park, South African Tourism; **93b** Stuffed Coelacanth, East London Museum, AA/C Sawyer; **94bl** Statue of a Victorian couple, Grahamstown, AA/P Kenward; **95b** Groot Constantia, AA/C Sawyer; **96/97** Whale Watching, Hermanus, AA/C Sawyer; **97c** Sunbird, Kirstenbosch, AA/P Kenward; **98** Mountain Zebra National Park, AA/C Sawyer; **99b** Cango caves, AA/P Kenward; **100t** Donkin Reserve, Port Elizabeth, AA/C Sawyer; **101tr** Rhodes Memorial, AA/C Sawyer; **102** Drostdy Museum, Swellendam, AA/C Sawyer; **103t** Ferry, Wild Coast, AA/C Sawyer; **103b** Haga-Haga, Wild Coast, AA/C Sawyer; **111** Warthog, Milwane Wildlife Sanctuary, Swaziland, AA/S McBride; **112/113** African Arts Centre, Durban, AA/S McBride; **113tr** African Arts Centre, Durban, AA/S McBride; **114l** City Hall, AA/P Kenward; **114/115c** Golden Mile, AA/S McBride; **116/117b** Hindu Temple, AA/C Sawyer; **117t** Hindu Temple, AA/C Sawyer; **119** Valley of a Thousand Hills, AA/C Sawyer; **120t** Globe Tavern, Barberton, AA/C Sawyer; **120/121b** Ox wagons, Blood River, AA/C Sawyer; **122t** Impala, AA/S McBride; **122/123b** White rhinoceros, Hluhluwe-Imfolozi National Park, AA/C Sawyer; **125** Pilgrim's Rest, AA/C Hampton; **126** Pilgrim's Rest, AA/S McBride; **127** Panning for gold, Pilgrim's Rest, AA/C Hampton; **128tr** Oribi Gorge, AA/P Kenward; **128cl** Sudwala Caves, AA/C Sawyer; **129b** Surfer, AA/P Kenward; **130** Shakaland, AA/S McBride; **133** Mantenga Cultural Village, Swaziland, AA/S McBride; **134/135b** Lesotho, AA/S McBride; **135t** Church congregation, Maseru, AA/S McBride; **143** Sandton shopping mall, Johannesburg, AA/P Kenward; **144/145** Skyline, Johannesburg, AA/C Sawyer; **146l** Gold Reef City, AA/P Kenward; **147t** Johannesburg Art Gallery, AA/M Birkitt; **148t** Museumafrica, AA/P Kenward; **149tr** Street performer, AA/C Sawyer; **149b** Market Theatre, courtesy Market Theatre; **150t** Stone Cottage, Parktown, AA/M Birkitt; **150/151b** Randberg Waterfront, AA/C Sawyer; **153** Soweto, AA/C Sawyer; **154** Near Hartbeespoort Dam, AA/S McBride; **156** Strijdom Square, Pretoria, AA/S McBride; **157** Melrose House, AA/S McBride; **158** Paul Kruger House Museum, AA/C Sawyer; **160** Union Buildings, AA/C Sawyer; **161** Frieze of the Great Trek of 1838, Voortrekker Monument, AA/C Sawyer; **167** Kalahari desert, AA/C Sawyer; **168t** City Hall, Kimberley, AA/C Sawyer; **169b** Kimberley Mine Museum, AA/C Sawyer; **170** Big Hole, Kimberley, AA/C Sawyer; **172** Augrabies Falls National Park, AA/C Sawyer; **173** City Hall, Bloemfontein, AA/C Sawyer; **174/175c** Gariep Dam, AA/S McBride; **175b** Golden Gate Highlands National Park, AA/S McBride; **176/177t** Kalahari desert, AA/C Sawyer; **178t** Elephants, Pilanesberg National Park, AA/S McBride; **179b** Sun City, AA/C Sawyer; **180/181** Golden Gate Highlands National Park, AA/S McBride.

Sight locator list

This index relates to the maps on the covers. We have given map references to the main sights of interest in the book. Grid references in italics indicate sights featured on town plans. Some sights within towns may not be plotted on the maps.

Dear Reader

Your comments, opinions and recommendations are very important to us. Please help us to improve our travel guides by taking a few minutes to complete this simple questionnaire.

You do not need a stamp (unless posted outside the UK). If you do not want to cut this page from your guide, then photocopy it or write your answers on a plain sheet of paper.

Send to: **The Editor, AA World Travel Guides,
FREEPOST SCE 4598, Basingstoke RG21 4GY.**

Your recommendations...

We always encourage readers' recommendations for restaurants, nightlife or shopping – if your recommendation is used in the next edition of the guide, we will send you a **FREE AA Guide** of your choice from this series. Please state below the establishment name, location and your reasons for recommending it.

_____

_____

_____

_____

_____

Please send me **AA Guide** _____

About this guide...

Which title did you buy?

AA _____

Where did you buy it? _____

When? m m / y y

Why did you choose this guide? _____

_____

_____

_____

_____

Did this guide meet your expectations?

Exceeded ☐   Met all ☐   Met most ☐   Fell below ☐

Were there any aspects of this guide that you particularly liked? _____

_____

_____

_____

continued on next page...

Is there anything we could have done better? _____
_____
_____
_____

About you...
Name (*Mr/Mrs/Ms*) _____
Address _____
_____
_____ Postcode _____
Daytime tel nos _____
Email _____

Please only give us your mobile phone number or email if you wish to hear from us about
other products and services from the AA and partners by text or mms, or email.

Which age group are you in?
Under 25 ☐ 25–34 ☐ 35–44 ☐ 45–54 ☐ 55–64 ☐ 65+ ☐

How many trips do you make a year?
Less than one ☐ One ☐ Two ☐ Three or more ☐

Are you an AA member? Yes ☐ No ☐

About your trip...
When did you book? m m / y y   When did you travel? m m / y y

How long did you stay? _____

Was it for business or leisure? _____

Did you buy any other travel guides for your trip? _____

If yes, which ones? _____
_____
_____

Thank you for taking the time to complete this questionnaire. Please send it to us as soon as
possible, and remember, you do not need a stamp (*unless posted outside the UK*).

AA Travel Insurance call 0800 072 4168 or visit www.theAA.com